Chronicles of Parenting: Book One

WHAT TO DO
with
God's
BEST GIFT

You have permission to parent

Jerry & Debbie Burbee

Published by Burbee Creations
https://BurbeeCreations.com

Printed in the United States of America

Paperback ISBN 978-1-64917-324-9

Hardcover ISBN 978-1-64917-350-8

eBook ISBN 978-1-64917-325-6

Editor: Michelle Schacht

Cover design by www.bookmarketinggraphics.com

We dedicate this book to our three children. We know that it is because of the lives they have chosen to live, honoring and serving God, that we were asked to write this book.

Chronicles of Parenting

A three-book series about how God raised our children.

BOOK ONE
What To Do With God's Best Gift

You have Permission to Parent

CONTENTS

FOREWORD

There has always been a call upon God's people, exhibited throughout history, and expressed in God's description of the children of Issachar to "understand the times to know how God's people should live" (1 Chronicles 12:32). This phrase has become a symbol for the importance of being aware of the culture around us so we can avoid the destruction from it's corrupted ideas and to experience God's better way of living

No matter at what point in human history, our enemy is working to "kill, steal, and destroy lives." At the same time, Jesus is moving to "give people life in the fullest way it can be lived" (John 10:10). In our generation there has been an all-out assault on God's design for family to the point that much of culture despises any idea of a traditional or Biblical family.

As creation drifts further and further away from God's design, and culture embraces more ungodly ideas there has been a corresponding bondage and destruction brought into the lives of children. Paul described it in Romans 1:18-32 as culture "suppresses the truth in unrighteousness...exchanges God's truth for lies...and given over to all kinds of lustful bondage." Right in the middle of this destructive chaos, God wants to raise up His better way in Jesus through the lives of His people.

Raising children is one of the most important, rewarding, and challenging experiences in life. Natural and spiritual parents, we have a unique opportunity to shape the lives of their children and help them become the best version of who God has made them to be. The Bible tells us in Proverbs 22:6, "Train up a child in the way he should go, even when he is old he will not depart from it." This verse highlights the importance of training our children according to God's ways.

Jerry and Debbie Burbee have not only raised three wonderful children but helped many others raise their own. They have gained much wisdom and insight in walking in God's design for parenting. In the pages of this book, " What Do We Do With God's Best Gift" they have done an excellent job of exploring God's design.

Throughout this book, Jerry and Debbie look at Biblical principles, and practical applications drawing from their own experiences that will help both natural and spiritual parents raise children in His life-giving ways. If you read this book you will gain precious insights of God that will strengthen and encourage you to follow God's design for parenting.

Doug Kreighbaum

INTRODUCTION TO CHRONICLES OF PARENTING

DEBBIE

I have often looked at my children, all three saved and passionately serving God, and said, "If all I do from now until eternity is thank God for their lives, it would still never be long enough." The Bible says in Psalm 127:3-5 that children are a reward from God and the one who has a quiver full is truly blessed (my paraphrase). I agree with this statement completely. In 2008, my husband and I felt God leading us to build a big house. I must say I was very content where I was but obedience has always been important to us. So we began to build our roughly 7,000 square foot house. We built it predominantly for the purpose of hospitality, which inspired us to name our new house, "The House of Blessing." Now, most people see the size of the house and think we call it our house of blessing because it is so big. The truth is they are very wrong. We call it our house of blessing because of the three amazing children God blessed us with who grew up in our home. We are truly blessed by these children and many others God has given us to love and help raise in our home.

When people began to encourage us about writing a book on parenting, I understood it was because of the lives my children live that brought about this honor more than anything we did. Thus, I want to start by first thanking God for their salvation and then saying thank you to my children for being obedient to His call. I would also like to say everything we did right in raising our children, we did by God's guidance through prayer. I know every child is individual, my three proved this, so the things God will show you about raising your children will be specific to them. I do not have the one and only blueprint for child rearing. What I do know is most of the principles in this book can guide you on your journey to your own house of blessing.

My only expertise is that I am a mom who read the promises God gave in His Word. I believed Him enough to pursue Him for the lives of my children, proving out His faithfulness to myself and to all His children who seek Him. I am not special in this. I am His child just as you are, and I know He loves you just as much as He loves me. I also know that what He has done for me He can and will do for you if you believe Him and pursue Him for the lives of your children.

As I prayed and began to write down the important topics I felt my husband and I needed to cover in this book, I thought it flowed well and was very excited by my original outline. Then I showed it to my husband. You see God has gifted me with a man who does not look at the world like I do. He began to rearrange things in a way that made sense to him. What we discovered together was that there are three main points which form the heart of this book supported by other principles that support and build upon each main idea. It was not until much later in our writing that our project blossomed into three books.

We have also seen through the years that we both have very unique ways of expressing our ideas. I am (for lack of a better description) a direct communicator who hold nothing back, and I write just like I would speak as if you were sitting with me. My husband is more of a poetic communicator, the real writer in the family. We have found there are people who need to hear things from my perspective and there are those who need to hear them from his, so we felt strongly that we must both write our parts in each chapter. I will say that we are in complete agreement with the things said by the other, and for the most part, Jerry tries, because he writes second, not to rewrite what I said but add to it, especially providing the dad's perspective.

My prayer is that as you read each book in this series the hope of God will fill your heart and you will see how much He longs to help us raise passionate children for His kingdom. The phrase you will hear me repeat a lot in the three books is: "If He did it for me, He will do it for you." This is because I want to be sure you believe it thoroughly, God wants His children to take Him at His word. He wants us to say, "Daddy, show me the way," and He wants to do just that. After all, it is really about our relationship with Him.

JERRY

My initial thought about being the author of a child rearing book is that it seemed very presumptuous, but as I thought and prayed about it, I was reminded of something God showed me many years ago about Christian how-to books and biographies. I read lots of books. I was constantly looking for the answers on how to live and do everything right. Being very legalistic in my relationship with God, I needed those answers. The books on prayer, on living righteously, on relationships, on stewardship, the biographies of the great men of faith—I read a bunch of them looking for the answers. I would try to recreate the methods suggested and often found myself failing at repeating their success. I would become discouraged and condemned because these books made it sound so easy and I was struggling. In the fog of this despair, I looked up at my bookshelf and prayed, "Why can't I do it like they do it? They make it sound so easy." A gentle breeze flowed through my soul with the insightful words, "Because you are not them." As I looked at the books on my shelves, the light came on. I could now see that all of these books were written from someone's experience. These books were notes from the diaries of other's encounters with God. They wanted to know how to pray or how to evangelize or how to have faith, and God took them through a process that was uniquely designed for them, then they wrote a book explaining their experience. The biographies were the stories of how God led them on their journey. None of these books are in the canon. None of them are the inspired Word of God. They are the stories of my brothers and sisters. I realize God was not wanting me to live their stories; He was wanting to give me my story.

With that in mind, I began to read the books differently. Instead of C. S. Lewis and Dietrich Bonhoeffer being the standard, they were suggestions. They were proof that God is able. During a think-and-synthesize yard mowing session, God began to illuminate different points, mix them with the scriptures I had been reading, and superimposed them over my current situations, and KA-POW! —I realized that the books were not the solution; they were part of my process. God was giving me my story.

The books Debbie and I are presenting are not the answer on how to raise children. They are a simulation of Debbie and I sitting in our living room with you and your spouse, talking about the wonderful things God did in our lives. Things He did. Things He changed in us. Things that turned our children towards Him. Things we would never have found if we had not gone to Him for help. Our hope and prayer is that our books can be another page in your story, and the story of your children.

SECTION ONE

GOD CHOSE YOU

This book has been broken into three sections that Jerry and I feel are the main points that we want to be sure you get from us. This first section contains chapters that we hope enforce the understanding that God Almighty has chosen you to be this child's parent and therefore **no one else** could do a better job. We feel each chapter in this section either speaks directly to that fact or is a consequence that comes from that fact.

CHAPTER 1

NO ONE BETTER THAN YOU

DEBBIE

For most of us the idea of becoming a parent is really exciting, especially with the first one. We call everyone we know. We show off our ultrasound pictures and begin planning a nursery. If there is hesitation, it is usually fear about the actual labor and delivery for mom, but not so much about caring for the baby.

Then it happens. We make it through labor and delivery and we are holding our little bundle of joy. Still not bad. We are busy taking pictures and entertaining our visitors when we're not trying to sleep. Then comes the fateful day when we have to leave the hospital and it happens—fear and doubt overwhelm us. Thoughts spring up like, "I don't know what to do with this baby! What if I mess this up? What were we thinking?" My husband was even afraid to hold our daughter except on a pillow because she was so little. "What if I break her?" he said.

If you think about it, this is the first time in your life you have been completely responsible for someone who cannot take care of themselves. This little bundle of joy is 100 percent dependent on you.

The devil loves these times in our lives where we feel vulnerable because his main weapon is his words. If he can get us to believe his lies, then he has power over us.

One of the lies I remember him telling me when my daughter was born was that she would end up on some talk show one day saying she was messed up because of her mom. That is why the Bible tells us we are to take every thought captive to Christ (2 Cor. 10:5). This is life-changing and life-freeing advice, because if we take these devil-generated thoughts and place them next to Jesus, the Living Word, we are able to fight. You see, I've never met a new parent who didn't find themselves facing doubts about their parenting abilities and these doubts then lead you to doubt that God knew what he was doing to make you a parent.

So the question we then have to answer is, "Is God really omniscient like the Bible says?" Let's first look at what omniscient even means. Dictionary.com defines omniscient as having complete or unlimited knowledge, awareness, or understanding; perceiving all things. The Bible is full of scriptures that support the conclusion that God is omniscient, and as such, He knows all things. Some examples include: 1 Samuel 2:3; 1 Chronicles 28:9; Acts 15:18; and Isaiah 46:9-10. God's omniscience includes knowing everything about the baby you are holding in your arms. The Bible goes on to tell us He even planned it that way.

The world would like us to believe that it was a flip of a coin; that by chance one of a million sperm cells happened to penetrate the random egg of the month and—BOOM—the dice was thrown and the child was determined.

Maybe the child you are holding was, in your mind, a mistake. Maybe your birth control failed, or you had a moment of passionate weakness and now you are going to be parenting this child all alone. The Word of God is very clear that no child is random or a mistake to Him. Psalms 139:13-14 says, "For You (speaking of God) created my innermost being. You knit me together in my mother's womb. I praise

You because I am fearfully and wonderfully made; Your works are wonderful, I know that full well." Now, that doesn't sound accidental or random at all. The Bible goes on to say that not only did He form that child, He called it. Galatians 1:15 states, "But God who set me apart from my mother's womb and called by His grace was pleased." Isaiah 49:1 reads, "Before I was born the Lord called me; from my mother's womb He has spoken my name." Lastly, Psalms 71:6 says, "From birth I have relied on You; You brought me forth from my mother's womb. I will ever praise you." These verses make it clear that God planned your child for a purpose. No child is an accident to God.

Agreeing that God planned this child, the next question is, "But what if He gave him to the wrong parent? Can I do this?" The Bible speaks to this as well. Genesis 33:5 says, "These are the children God has graciously given me." Psalms 127:3,5 explains further: "Children are a heritage from the Lord, offspring a reward from Him. Blessed is the man whose quiver is full. They will not be put to shame when they contend with their opponents in the court." God even speaks all the way to your grandchildren in Proverbs 17:6: "Children's children are a crown to the ages, and parents are the pride of their children."

The devil would have you believe that the universe got this all wrong and you are going to mess this parenting thing all up. But the truth from God's Word says He created your baby in a very specific way and He created you to be that baby's parent. No one else in the whole world was meant to be your child's parent. In truth, you are the perfect parent for the child you now hold. He or she was not an accident or a mistake. Our omniscient God does not do that. Even if you adopted the child you now hold, God's omniscience covers that too. So take a deep breath and slowly let it out. Tell the devil to shut up. Tell the devil you are going to believe God.

God does not make mistakes. He knows every little detail about your child. He intricately pieced together that delicate DNA strand so that your baby would have the unique characteristics he has. He did the same for you when you were in your own mother's womb. Then, in His ultimate wisdom, He said this child He created needed you to be his parent. You were created for this. That means you, my friend, with all your insecurities and personality quirks, are the absolute perfect parent for your child. For anything you come up against, God's reply is you are the right person for this job. It doesn't matter if your child is be a genius and you feel average., God says you got this! Same if your child has a learning disability. It still doesn't matter. You are the best parent for this child. Boy or girl, no matter what personality or physical characteristics your child has, God picked you.

Some of your traits were given to you precisely so you would have what you needed for your child. You may have at times even wondered why God made you like He did or why He has allowed you to have some of the struggles or experiences you have had in life, but unlike us, God sees the whole picture. I see only today and have no idea what tomorrow may hold, but God does. Even your struggles were preparing you for this child. God has been forming you into the perfect parent for this child your whole life. I hope I've emphasized my point thoroughly here, that God chose you to be this child's parent and that no one in the whole earth would be a better parent for him than you.

One reason this point needs to be clear in your heart is that in America, even the American church, we are notorious for comparing ourselves with others. We need to stop looking around and measuring ourselves with others. We need to stop looking around and measuring ourselves with Susie Homemaker next door. Stop comparing yourself to that elder's wife. You see, we seem to have an obsession with our neighbor. We really know nothing about them, but we are somehow sure they have a better life, better stuff, and a perfect family. Most of us would be shocked to know the truth—that they have the same struggles and insecurities that we do.

Peter struggled with this comparison game too. In John 21, Jesus and Peter were having this great future revealing moment where Jesus was telling Peter the type of death he would have as an old man before. Then Peter sees John and says, "Lord, what about him?" Jesus's reply in John 21:22 was, "If I want him to remain alive until I return, what is that to you? You must follow me." When we are busy looking at our neighbor, it is impossible to keep our eyes on Jesus. Jesus made your child. Jesus gave you that child to raise. If Jesus had wanted your neighbor to raise your child, He was perfectly capable of making that happen. After all He is God. Your responsibility is to be faithful to God for the child God gave you. Jesus's words to Peter, "You must follow Me," are just as true for us as they were for Peter. After all, Jesus carries the instruction manual to your child's heart, personality, and calling.

In my children's lives, when walking them through the highs and lows, successes and failures, calling out to Jesus was key. He helped raise my children. I cannot stress enough the importance of calling out to Him for everything you need concerning them. Daddy God created them, Daddy God adores them, and He cares more then we realize about every little detail of their lives. He wants you and I to ask for His guidance and help. Whenever I called out to Him, He never failed me, and it is exactly that fact from my experience that makes me so certain He will do the same for you. I am special to God but so are you and so is your child. What I've experienced in my life is not unique; it is just who God is. He loves His children, and the Bible says He has a faithfulness that endures forever. Take Him at His word.

I am not saying you won't have times where you feel stuck. My daughter was such a good debater of issues even at three years old. I used to have to remind myself I was the adult, and as such, knew what was best. It is a very common problem for new parents to doubt their ability. You can bet the devil wants you to think you cannot do it. He will tell you everyone else could do it better. Well, he lies. The devil is a liar. I choose which voice I will listen to. I can believe a big, fat liar or I can believe a loving, omniscient God. God believed in you enough to trust you with His precious gift. That's the voice I want to trust.

JERRY

If no one has said it to you yet, let me be the one to get things started.

You have permission to parent.

I remember being a new parent, and I have watched young parents as they struggle with the same thing. It's like we need somebody to tell us it is okay to be the parent.

I'll say it again: **You have permission to parent.**

I think I can say this with the authority of a father, a fellow citizen, and as a representative of God: this world needs you to parent. Your fears and hesitations are common and can be overwhelming. But as Debbie mentioned, you are the parent that God chose for this child.

Let's break it down.

"You" - Not someone else. You.

"Have permission" - You are authorized by God to fulfill the role of parent in this child's life. (If needed, make yourself a badge and wear it proudly. "I am an official, authorized parent.") You were involved in bringing this child into the world, therefor you get to guide and train this child as it experiences the world. You will make mistakes. You will drop her on her head (or maybe I'm the only one who has done that). But God is able to provide all that is needed to love her. That's what permission is. You have been approved to love this child as God has loved you.

"To parent" - First, you have to eliminate all the bad, wrong images of parenting that fill your head. You've seen them in movies. You've experienced them with your own parents. You have seen it done to others. You do not have to follow these models. But, with grace and humility, you do need to identify what is good and what is bad. The standard to use is not necessarily another human; the real model for parenting is Father God.

What we are trying to recreate for our kids is what God has done for us. He is patient but firm. He provides for all our needs but doesn't give us everything we want. His love includes discipline that is full of grace and mercy, yet holds us accountable. To see clearly how the Father cares for us, we have to know Him and His Word. As we grow in knowing Him, we become doers of the Word, not just hearers. Our actions will reflect the faith we have in what He has said.

Sometimes, I look back at my younger self and sadly shake my head. For most of my childhood, and into my young adult years, I wanted God to pick me to do something great. I wanted to make my mark on the world, and knew that if God picked me, it would happen. All-star athlete? World-renowned physician? Award winning songwriter? Strangely enough, those are not the paths God chose. With my eyes on the horizon, rather than on Him, I nearly missed it. What could be greater than God trusting me to raise a little girl that loves Him and was determined to love Him for her whole life? What could be greater than God entrusting to me the training of two boys to become men that chose Him and refused the world?

"But, God, as a celebrity, I would have everyone's attention and thousands would be impacted. Wouldn't that be a better use of my life?" I ruminate on those words now and get stuck between vomiting and crying. What was I thinking?

I used to comfort myself with, "When you finally get the kids out of the house, then you will have time to focus on the important stuff."

Are you kidding me?! If I could go back to my younger self, I am afraid I would punch him in the face. God did choose me for something great.

The gospels reveal that Jesus interacted with the crowds, but His focus was on the Twelve and those close to Him. Through His life and His teaching, He helped them to see the Father and to discern the difference between the so-called good things of the earth and the true riches of heaven. The crowds wanted to make Him king, and they flocked to Him to experience His miracles. His own family and disciples tried to convince Him that His impact on the world could be greater if He catered to the crowds and the important people. They shooed away the children because He was not to be bothered by such lowly ones. Yet, He wanted them to come near so He could touch them. He did not need the approval of the crowd to acknowledge His worth or to validate His actions. He understood that investing in those whom the Father had given Him was much more important than impressing the crowd. Jesus revealed the Father's heart by "raising" the disciples to seek and to know the Father's heart. God chose you and me for greatness by entrusting us to raise our children to know Him.

God chose you. He trusts you.

For me it was easier to think about God using me for something "big" because it was always far enough away that I didn't have to worry about it really happening. The "big thing" comforted my ego and allowed me to avoid what I really feared—me. I never had much confidence that I could actually do "the great thing" because I seemed to always make one mistake after another. Being concerned about success was another way of me saying I needed everyone else to validate me. If I did the "big thing" and was famous, that would mean a lot of other people thought I was successful. If you haven't realized it yet, securing the approval of others is like catching the wind. You can feel its movement, but when it stops blowing, you have nothing to hold onto. Always looking to the horizon allows the comfort of someday "I will" without it ever being challenged.

That same fear of failure can restrain us from embracing the "big things" that God has brought to us. That fear originates in our lack of faith in God and manifests in disobedience and grumbling. The journey of the Israelites out of Egypt demonstrates God's dislike for disobedience and grumbling. He confronts these attitudes vehemently because He hates seeing us deprived of what He has for us. He does not wish for His people to be trapped by lies. To assume God would bring something into our lives that He has not provided the ability for us to conquer insults His character. Fear that we can't, or that He won't, ensures failure before any effort is exerted.

Thankfully, God's grace to me, and for my children, alleviated what normally crippled me. Somehow I knew I had what it took to be a father. We all have battles that distract us from agreeing with God's grace, fortunately this one was not intense for me. I say this as my boast in the Lord. I don't know how I was able to be elevated from my normal life of fear and find the confidence to be a father. I say this to stir your faith towards this confidence. If He did it for me, He can do it for you.

God chose you.

He trusts you.

You can do it because of Him.

You have permission to parent.

You have a heavenly authorization to love those children the way God has loved you.

You can do it.

CHAPTER 2
CHILD OF THE MOST HIGH GOD

DEBBIE

As Christians, we believe there will be a day of judgment. On that day, I will stand before the Almighty God and give an account for how I lived my life, an account as to how I used the many gifts or talents He gave me. I will stand all by myself. I won't be able to say to God that anyone else in the world was responsible for what I did with my life and how I treated others but me. This may seem like a strange way to start a section entitled Child of the Most High God, but for me it makes perfect sense. The child God placed in my home is in some ways a loaner. You see, this child really is God's child and He has loaned His child to me with great trust that I will love and care for him just as He would. One day, I will stand before Him and give an account for the way I handled this amazing gift He bestowed upon me.

Psalms 127:3 says that my children are a reward from the Lord. They were His children but He gave them to me as a reward. I am to live and care for them just like He did. Galatians 1:15 says He set them apart in my womb and called them. Isaiah 49:1 says, "He has spoken their names." This perfect little gift you are holding came from God because James 1:17 says every good and perfect gift comes from the Lord. The point I am making here is that even though our children are a gift from God to us for a time, first and foremost, they belong to Him.

Deuteronomy 4:24 describes God as a jealous God. I wonder if we paused to think before every action we took and remembered it is going to be done to one of God's own treasured possessions, would our actions change? Well, I hope that all my actions show Christ this, but sadly, I often fall short of my Christ-likeness goal, usually due to my selfishness. Thankfully, He is also a God who allows for repentance along with second chances, so we can repent to our children and make things right when we miss the mark.

Jesus, our representative of the Father, loved children. He said His kingdom was made up of such as these and His disciples should not ever stop them from coming to Him. Luke 18:16 specifically says, "But, Jesus called the children to Him and said, 'Let the little children come to me, and do not hinder them, for the kingdom of God belongs to such as these.'" Matthew 19:14 and Mark 10 agree. In Mark 10, Jesus was mad at His disciples, and Mark 10:14 says He was indignant. Let's read it: "People were bringing little children to Jesus for Him to place His hands on them, but the disciples rebuked them. When Jesus saw this He was indignant. He said to them, 'Let the little children come to me and do not hinder them for the kingdom of God belongs to such as these.'" You see, Jesus knew these parents got it. They were bringing their children to Him because they knew He was the source of blessing for them too.

Matthew 18:6 says, "If anyone causes one of these little ones—those who believe in me to stumble, it would be better for them to have a large millstone hung around their neck and to drown in the sea." Jesus wanted to be sure we understand how serious the Father is about His children. God loves each and every one of them. This verse in Matthew 18 and later in Mark 9 are both addressed to anyone who makes a child stumble, which relates to us as parents since we have the greatest influence over our kids' lives, especially in the first formative years. Ephesians 6:4 says, "Fathers do not exasperate your children, instead bring him up in the training and instruction of the Lord." Colossians 3:21 says, "Fathers, do not embitter your children or they will become discouraged." The word "wrath" , also translated as exasperate, Ephesians 6 according to *Ellicott's Bible Commentary for English Readers* "denotes an aspiration by arbitrary and unsympathetic rule." Matthew Henry, a Bible scholar who is known for his commentaries, goes on to say, "The duty of parents: Be not impatient, use no unreasonable servitude, deal prudently and wisely with children...bring them up well, under proper and compassionate correction and in the knowledge of the duty God requires." Look back over what Ellicott and Henry are saying, and then meditate on what God is saying to us as parents.

I like to use 1 Corinthians 13 to be sure my definition of love looks like God intends it to because, let's face it, our culture has really messed up our idea of what love is. In 1 Corinthians 13: 4-7 God defined love for us, and the definition doesn't resemble our current day version at all because it speaks of kindness, being forgiving, not being selfish or boastful and more. I read it often so I can spot the real from the counterfeit. Then the Bible tells us the Holy Spirit lives in His children so that means we can personify God's definition of love to our children through the same Spirit.

Having such a serious responsibility from God as to how He expects me to raise and love the children He has given me would be overwhelming if I did not understand that God is the one who helps me complete this very task. I already have established that this omniscient God chose you because you are the exact one to raise this child. Yes, He holds you accountable, but He also is the very one who empowers you to do it. God has trusted you to bring this child up to know His one true Father God. The Bible says God will never leave you or forsake you (Heb. 13:5). Yes, He is very serious about His children but remember where your help really comes from. Do not neglect to spend time with God because the more you know Him the more like Him you become.

Your children are counting on you.

JERRY

We can be secure in the fact that we are the chosen parents for our children. However, we also need to have a bit of fear and trepidation at how serious our role is. The sober and serious thoughts of our accountability need not be lost for they are important. If you are like me, hearing that you are raising a "Child of the Most High God" creates a little bit of anxiety. Your thoughts may be like mine were: "Whoa, I was nervous enough knowing I was responsible for caring for another human being. Now I'm under the scrutiny of how I take care of God's treasured possession. Uh, that wonderful thought doesn't relieve the anxiety at all."

In the past when I read Joshua 1:7-9 (NIV) below, it used to give me palpitations. Let me use my experience with this passage to illustrate how I have found some balance with fear and confidence.

Be strong and very courageous. Be careful to obey all the law my servant Moses gave you; do not turn from it to the right or to the left, that you may be successful wherever you go. Keep this Book of the Law always on your lips; meditate on it day and night, so that you may be careful to do everything written in it. Then you will be prosperous and successful. Have I not commanded you? Be strong and courageous. Do not be afraid; do not be discouraged, for the Lord your God will be with you wherever you go.

Joshua is getting ready to do something very important. He will be leading God's people into their new land. This situation is similar to being a parent. We are doing something very important. We are leading someone into a new land.

Here's my list of what Joshua was supposed to do:

1. Be strong.
2. Be very courageous.
3. Be careful to obey all of the law.
4. Do not turn from it, to the right or left.

5. If you turn to the left or right from it, you will not be successful.
6. Keep it on your lips.
7. Meditate on it day and night.
8. Be careful to do everything written in it if you want to be prosperous and successful.
9. Do not be afraid.
10. Do not be discouraged.

When I would read Joshua 1:7-9 and contemplate the list of all the things he was supposed to do, I could see God having the same conversation with me. It created panic. I thought I was supposed to conjure up all the strength and moxy to create all those qualities in myself by myself. God laid a heavy responsibility on me and now I had to figure out how to do it. It lead to worries like:

"How am I supposed to do that? All the time?"

"How do I make myself strong right now?"

"What if I wander to the right or to the left, will I be lost forever? Is there no way to recover?"

You probably already have a similar list of how you are supposed to raise your child. Here's a sample one:

1. Teach them to love God.
2. Teach them to be respectful.
3. Do not let them become brats.
4. You are responsible for their wellbeing twenty-four hours a day, seven days a week for the next eighteen years.
5. Raise them appropriately so you are not responsible for them longer than twenty years.
6. Love them.
7. Let them know they are special.
8. There are probably a lot of other things, but I don't know what they are.
9. Etc.

Lists like these made me as comfortable as having a wasp's nest near my front door. Something is going to get me. Then God showed me an important phrase I had missed when reading Joshua 1:7-9: "...for the Lord your God will be with you wherever you go."

Boom! THAT is the anxiety crusher. THAT is how we raise a Child of The Most High God.

I do need a fear and respect of God that causes me to listen to what He says. I need to study and meditate on His words. I need to be diligent to observe His commands. But being strong and courageous and doing all of these things is not based on my abilities, they are based on His presence. I thought God was telling Joshua to suck it up and be a man and stop being afraid and do what he had been told. Instead, God was telling Joshua that since He will be with Him, he could be strong and courageous. My paraphrase of Joshua 1: 7-9 would be;

"I am with you. Linger in My words; live them. If you do not stray from Me, there is no reason to be afraid. The land is yours, because I said so."

Joshua was able to have confidence because God would always be with Him. That same confidence is ours to claim as we raise our children. Having a fear of God that brings respect is healthy. Being confident that you can be successful raising your child is also healthy. This fear and confidence do not need to be opposed to each other.

After I overcame the anxiety, this aspect of parenting brought me the most joy. It was such a privilege to awaken and direct my children towards the Father. As they each made their own connection with Jesus and surrendered to being led by the Spirit, well, I cannot think of anything else that has been as satisfying. Knowing that He was with us, I had the confidence to actively participate in the process and see the touch of the Father transform each selfish, rebellious monster into a Child of the Most High God. It has been awesome.

Looking back and remembering what has happened reminds me of how my dad described woodcarving. If he was carving a figure, he would take a block of wood and cut it into the rough shape of his desired figure, like a dog or a person. At this stage, he revealed a glimpse of what it was going to be, though of course it lacked the details that made it come alive or reflect any personality; it lacked the beautiful touch of the artisan's hands. When asked how he was able to take a rough block of wood and turn it into something so beautiful, he would take his pipe out of his mouth and, with an ornery gleam in his eye, point to the piece of wood and say, "Well, I just look at this here piece of wood and see what I want to make out of it and then whittle away the parts that don't need to be there." That is how I view child rearing.

Each child is a precious work of art, awaiting to be released from its prison. The layers of rebellion and selfishness need to be masterfully removed so that a Child of the Most High God can be displayed. Though integral to the process, I was not the master craftsman. God alone has the vision and the skill to create a masterpiece; I was simply the knife He used to bring shape to what He had already seen. My part of this process was to discipline and encourage, shaving away the worthless parts, as He formed my children into a reflection of His glory.

A knife is the most important tool a wood carver has to create his piece of art. Nothing is worse for a carver than to have a dull knife. Instead of cleanly removing each sliver of wood, a dull knife tears the wood, leaving ugly marks that deform the piece. As a result, my dad knew how to sharpen a knife. When the knife was not performing as expected, he would lay down the block of wood and begin to sharpen his knife. He had a stone that he would spit on, or wet with some oil, and slowly move the knife back and forth. After a few strokes, he would look at the edge, feel it with his thumb, and maybe even try to shave a few hairs off his arm. Next, he would move it across a piece of leather which had been treated with jeweler's rouge to get an even finer edge. When satisfied, he returned to the carving. Since his goal was to shape the piece of wood, the knife was only useful if it stayed sharp. For him there was nothing more frustrating than trying to work with a knife that couldn't keep an edge.

A child of the Most High God is a masterpiece created by the Master. We are merely the tools He uses to bring shape and definition to His artistry. If we are dull and ineffective for the work, the Master turns His attention to sharpening our edge and removing anything that might prevent us from being effective. Our resistance to being sharpened, or lack of resolve to stay sharp, can potentially damage what He plans to create.

This child is yours to raise. It is a daunting task, but we can be strong and courageous. The Lord is with us wherever we go. The Master's hand is upon you to skillfully shape this child into HIs image. Will you let the Master do His work in you so you can aid Him in doing His work in your child? A child of the Most High God awaits your answer.

CHAPTER 3
SPEAK LIFE

DEBBIE

In this chapter, I want to talk about the power our words carry. The Bible tells us our words carry the power of life and death in them. Think about it for a moment. We can say that it was our sin that put Jesus on the cross, but in that moment it was really words that put Him there. The words came out of sinful hearts, but the crowd yelling "crucify Him" was the power that moved Pilot's hand. When Jesus healed or brought Lazarus back to life, He did that with His words too. When we talk to or about someone, the words we use carry enormous power. That fact is true about everything we say whether we like it or not, and it is especially true when it comes to our children.

It would be impossible to talk about our words without talking about the book of James. It is full of scriptures we will talk about, so I recommend you first read the book of James. It is a short book and won't take you long to read but it is powerful.

Now that you've read James, let's continue. In James 3:2, it says if we could control our tongues, we would be perfect, and also could control ourselves in every way: "We all stumble in many ways. Anyone who is never at fault in what they say is perfect, able to keep their whole body in check." Sometimes our children can challenge us in this to our very

JERRY AND DEBBIE BURBEE

limit. G.K. Chesterson, a Bible scholar and apologist in the early 1900's, says that children exult in monotony. So when your child reaches one of those stages we all have seen, like the "No" stage, the "Why?" Stage, or the "Mine" stage and you are trying to fulfill the demands of your busy schedule that monotony can make you feel like you are losing your mind. This is precisely when having the self-control of the Spirit is so important.

James would say is the very moment we must control our tongue because words said in frustration carry as much weight as our best thought out praise. How many of you have something a parent or a sibling yelled at you in frustration that still rings in your head? Maybe it was a name you were called or an embarrassment that followed the event. I personally was blessed with my father's very prominent nose and as you could guess the teasing I took from other not-so-kind children could be very hurtful. In fact, it was so hurtful that until I was in nursing school and actually saw what takes place in a nose reconstruction surgery I was sure I would someday have mine made smaller. After watching that surgery, I decided my nose wasn't so bad. My cowardness still did not change the fact that most of my life I was very self-conscious about it, and I must admit I prayed hard that none of my children would inherit this physical characteristic from me. (Thank you again, Jesus, for answering that prayer.) You see, words carry power. My words can bring harm or they can produce life. Most people who have great accomplishments in their lives almost always have a cheerleader who loves them and tells them they can accomplish anything.

Some researchers say it takes a minimum of five positive encounters to change the effects caused by one negative one. Dr Phil McGraw, a well-known talk show host during my years, says it takes a hundred. I don't know about you but I tend to agree with Dr. Phil. Five encounters sure seems to be setting the bar a little low, but then again I am very sensitive to words.

The Bible is very clear that our words carry power. James 3:6 states, "The tongue also is a fire, a world of evil among the parts of the body. It corrupts the whole body, sets the whole course of one's life on fire, and is itself set on fire by hell." James goes on to say it is a restless evil, full of deadly poison, and verse 9 says, "With it we curse those who have been made in the image of God." That should put the fear of God in all of us because every man was made in God's image.

Our relationship with our child is one of the most influential relationships we will ever have. Most of us care very deeply about what we believe our parents think of us. We want to know they are proud of us. When we are little, it may come as praise for that first step. When we are in school, it may be wanting them to recognize our new talents, like art work, or to be proud of our grades. I would go so far as to say we never lose that, and neither do our children. Sadly, I have watched many adult children dealing with parents who are suffering with the brutal disease of Alzheimer's. If you don't know, Alzheimer's is a disease that robs a person of their memories but also can completely change a person's personality too. It can take a mild-mannered, little old Christian lady and make her cuss like a sailor. To the child of this little old lady, it can be extremely distressing to see their once mild-mannered loving mother change and yell obscenities at them. Even though they know it is the disease instead of their mother, it is still a horrible thing to process. Our children are no different. They need to know, meaning we need to say, we are absolutely overjoyed by who they are. This never changes, so whether you have a toddler or adult children your words still carry power over them.

Speak life over your children. Never, never, never speak death. Speaking life totally changes everything for your child. When I was young, my mother was so great at making sure I knew I was loved and lovable that I was honestly dumb founded to find out someone didn't like me. Our children need to walk into this life knowing you and Daddy God absolutely adore them and believe in God's call over them. When someone else speaks death over them, you should be the first to dispel the lie of the enemy over them and replace those lies with words of life. Be especially sure you speak the words that the Bible says about them because it is the strongest truth we have when it comes to dispelling the enemy's lies.

We choose who we want to partner with as we raise our children. Satan, the accuser of the brethren, wants you to agree with him. He wants you to be his mouth piece. God forbid! I pray I always partner with God in what I speak over the children He gave me.

What I speak has a way of revealing my own heart. The Bible tells us that what is in our hearts will overflow out of our mouths (my paraphrase of Matthew 11:34 and Matthew 15:18). Luke 6:45 says basically that a good person out of the good of his heart produces good and an evil person out of his evil heart produces evil. Our hearts become good or evil by what we fill them with and who we surround them by. That is true for us and will become important in training our children too. So guard your heart.

Then ask the Holy Spirit to help you to use self control as you do speak. The Bible places self-control as a fruit of the Spirit and it places fits of rage as a work of the flesh. My encouragement for you is to pray for the Holy Spirit to produce self-control in you. Then be diligent to allow Him to produce it in you. Remember, what we feed lives. So if you are struggling with your flesh, do a real-life examination around what you are feeding yourself. You may also need to have a talk with God about your busy schedule and see how many things you have taken on that He is not asking of you. Let God overhaul you completely if need be, and if you have been too busy to spend time in God's presence, then I guarantee it is time for an overhaul. I can say this from personal experience. Not having time with God and filling yourself with the wrong things will always cause you to say and do the things that you will need to repent of later, so make the change.

Feed yourself on worship and the Word of God. Then do as Deuteronomy 11:18-21 says,

Fix these words of Mine in your hearts and minds; tie them as symbols on your hands and bind them on your foreheads. Teach them to your children, talking about them when you sit at home and when you walk along the road, when you lie down, and when you get up. Write them on the door frames of your houses and on your gates. So that your days and the days of your children may be many in the land the Lord swore to give your ancestors, as many as the days the heavens are above the earth.

I am very serious about this scripture. I constantly tell my children of the goodness of God and of what God , and I, think of them. I call my sons and my son-in-love handsome princes and powerful men of God. I bought rings for my daughter and my daughter-in-love that are crowns to help remind them that they are princesses of the Most High God. I want them all to know the truth of what God says over them. I do not care if I even embarrass them by how loud I cheer because it is my job to speak the love of God and my own love over them. For I know the plans my God has for them. They are "plans to give them a hope and a future" (Jer. 29:11).

JERRY

The way I found to speak life into my children began with confronting this disturbing fact about parenting: your children are going to grow up with deficiencies, scars, and quirks that are of your making. Your parenting will cause them issues that only the Holy Spirit and counseling can resolve. The best you can hope to do is to limit the amount of garbage and the type of baggage they have when they leave your house.

No matter what you do, your kids are going to grow up having problems. You are going to make mistakes. They are not going to be as level headed as you had hoped. They will discover that what you taught them about the world is not sufficient for the world they encounter. Although this may seem rather negative, I found it helpful to acknowledge this dark side of reality.

I had times when I was so scared of mistakes that it would nearly paralyze me. I would think, "Oh no, I made a mistake. Is this the scar that will define them for the rest of their life?" or "Wouldn't it be better not to do anything rather than screwing up and wrecking their life?" A dozen different versions of these statements haunted me. Straining to be perfect is one of the battles that has been a constant in my life. Always failing. Never good enough. I had to accept failure as part of the process of life and parenting. Yet, I realized my words would shape their image of who they are and how they would interact with the world. If I demanded perfection from them and myself, those words would perpetuate lies. If I did nothing and said nothing, I would leave a void that would be filled with the pain of absent love.

Realizing this truth has helped me in three ways:

1. No matter how hard I try, I am not going to be perfect.
2. Knowing that I am going to mess them up any way, I get to choose the manner in which they are messed up.
3. The words I speak fill their hearts with images that will guide them for the rest of their lives.

Let me explain each of these further.

As the Father walked with me into fatherhood, He showed me that as long as I would give Him opportunity, He would take my imperfections and create His glory through them. "My grace is sufficient. My power is made perfect in weakness" (1 Cor. 12:9). If I remained humble and followed as best I could, He would take care of the rest. The relief of knowing that my best attempts to be perfect would not be successful and that my straining to try to prove that I was perfect would actually create more problems gave me the freedom to be a father. I saw in myself (and observed in other parents as well) that the labor needed to remain perfect causes a stiff environment that is unrealistic and caustic. Children make lots of mistakes. What better way to show them how to deal with their mistakes than to expose my mistakes and demonstrate healthy ways to cope with them? When I tried to hide imperfections, or tried to have the appearance of flawlessness, the only person who was fooled was me. My wife, my kids, and seemingly everyone else saw right through my charade and pitied me for it. I think this attempt at perfection creates a lot of garbage and increases the amount of baggage children have to deal with. It's not real, and it helps no one. I spoke life over my home and into my children by being real. I tried hard to do the best I could, but I also laughed at my own mistakes. I laughed when they noticed my mistakes. We laughed at their mistakes. I apologized for when I did something wrong or painful. I expected them to do the same. Speaking life means saying the words that are real and right. They needed to hear what the Father, and this father, thought of them. They needed to hear from me that they were loved and that they were wonderful, even when they were horrible. If I went too far when I teased them about a mistake, I tried to go back and apologize and clarify my love for them. As I matured as a father, I stopped teasing and tried to help them find their own humor in any horrible situation. I wanted them to know that life is not about perfection; it is about living, and living doesn't always go smoothly.

Laugh when we can.

Cry when we need to.

Apologize frequently.

Love like crazy.

And always trust that God is in control.

Speaking life is demonstrated by living in God's reality. Things are as God says they are. Speaking life uses faith and hope to identify things as they are from God's perspective and spits in the face of a world that seeks to keep us blind.

Knowing that I was going to screw them up anyway gave me the release to decide how I was going to mess with them. It let me say, "What am I going to build?"

The two rules I stressed were:

1. Obedience and respect.
2. Have fun.

To me these are the two essential sides of the parenting coin; they have to be in balance. Parenting that stresses obedience and respect without any humor can be harsh and critical. Focusing only on having fun without respect and obedience creates hedonistic brats. Both are

25

important doorways to speaking life. Letting a child be disobedient or disrespectful sets them on course for death. Likewise, only having fun without any boundaries sets a course to destruction. Life comes from speaking what is real. God's standards and God's nature are real, and they are what brings life. Correcting a child to keep them perfect (and to appear that you are perfect as a parent) focuses on image and the perception of others and is a direct path to bad parenting. Correcting a child with words of life brings a straightening to what is crooked and turns them back to God. Harsh, demoralizing comments that try to shame a child into better behavior do not bring life, although for the moment it might change behavior. Obedience and respect are formed through obedience and respect. If I do not respect my children in the way I talk to them, my words might be corrective but they will not bring life. If I shame, degrade, and humiliate in efforts to change them, the only change that will come is a hardened heart. If I demonstrate a lack of respect, I will reap what I have sown. Even though they have a snotty nose, dirty pants, and a bad attitude, all children deserve to be treated like a child of the Most High. If I stumble and yell at them, words of life given in an apology can help to restore the respect. Our obedience and respect in fulfilling the mandate to parent are displayed in the words we use to speak to our children and in the words used to speak about our children.

Fun comes because everyone likes to have fun. Laughter is more pleasant than sour faces. I found it very important that my children knew exactly what they had done that was inappropriate and they knew what steps were to be taken to correct the situation. My desire was that they would see this as gaining something better rather than having lost something. I wanted them to see that living God's way was best, and therefore, more fun. Things that disrespected others or broke the rules was only going to hurt someone, especially them. If I could point out how it was better to live according to God's nature, it was easier to have fun. The joy of our salvation is not merely that we get to go to heaven; it also involves getting to enjoy life here on earth without the bondage of sin.

Speaking words of life involves everything I say, why I say them, and the manner in which they are said. If I focus on living a life of obedience, respect, and fun with the Father at the head, it is much easier to live that way with my children. If I remember that God's way is always better, I can enjoy the fruit of life with Him, unhindered by the bondage of sin. As I demonstrate a life not focused on perfection, but one that keeps step with the Spirit, I will have freedom. This freedom can then be shared with my children. The words of life God has spoken over me, I can speak over them.

CHAPTER 4
CELEBRATE THEM

DEBBIE

Celebrate your child. Some of you might be asking what is she talking about. I don't want to make any assumptions here that you automatically know what I mean when I say to celebrate your child. Most of us think celebrating someone means an event like throwing a party for someone when they have had a great accomplishment, like getting a promotion at work. What I am talking about is a much broader definition of this. I'm talking about making sure your child knows everything about them is unique and wonderful. We usually understand that our children should be celebrated when they do something great, but I'm saying that we need to celebrate them every day just because they are a gift from God containing great value. Yes, praise them when they win a race or get an award but what I'm saying is take it far beyond that. Make sure they understand that you enjoy who they are and never assume they just know how you feel. Chances are if you are not telling them how much you admire and love them, they don't automatically know it.

When you meet me it will not take long for you to realize I am crazy about my children. As far as I can tell from the way the Bible talks about God, He feels the same way about His children. I know I could never love the way that I do if it were not for the way God has loved me. The Bible says in 1 John 3:1 that God has great love and that He lavishes it upon us. Don't get me wrong, the Bible also makes no indication that God is a pushover either. He expects His children to obey. In Galatians 6:7 it says, "Do not be deceived, God cannot be mocked. A man reaps what he sows." Therefore, I want to talk about the importance of celebrating your children. I believe that celebrating your children includes being someone who holds tight to rules, boundaries, and obedience. In fact, the next chapter is on making your children obey. Jerry and I struggled about the order of these two chapters. I do believe in extravagant love for your children. They need to know that in this world there are at least two people (Mom and Dad) who love them like crazy. They also need to know they have a Daddy God who loves them even more perfectly than us. However, true love does not mean spoiling them by letting them do anything they want without boundaries. True love has guidelines for them just as God has shown us by the way He loves.

The Bible says I can enter boldly into the throne room of God. Galatians 4:1-7 talks about how I am a daughter of the Lord and the Spirit of God makes it so I can cry out, "Abba Father (Daddy God)." I am an heir. The Bible says I can run to the presence of God yelling, "Daddy, I'm here!" I don't know about your experience, but I love, love, love the presence of God, and I have never left my time in God's presence feeling terrible about myself. I leave His presence feeling cherished and loved., Even after being corrected, I always feel like I can conquer the world.

My children may intermittently get praise from the people of the world, but more than likely, they will face a slaughter out there. Most children will struggle with self-esteem problems. But, when they walk through my door or into my presence I want them to know they are wanted, number one, and that I see who they are and absolutely love and support them.

People tell me my face glows when I see my kids, grandkids, or in-law kids. That is true. I do glow. I cannot wait to tell them how wonderful they are! It is truth spoken in love. Jerry and I use that phrase to talk about correction, and I am saying even my correction needs to leave them knowing they are loved. The Bible tells us that when we repent of our sins that God casts them as far as the east is from the west. I can't even calculate where that place is, so to me that means gone forever. We may have to live with the consequences of that sinful action, but God will not still be angry at us or make sure we know He is still angry by making us miserable. No, it is over. When you read the stories of the great men of God who fell into sin you do not ever see God throwing that repented of sin back in their face. It is done; the consequence has been paid so God never brings it up again.

Far too many times we as parents have too long a memory when it comes to something our child has done that made us angry, and unlike God, we don't let it go. However, we need to let them walk out their repentance as a new creation the same way God does with us. I actually heard a mom say, "Get out of here, I don't even want to look at you, I am so mad," to her child. That certainly does not fit into my definition of celebrating them. Celebrate them means that when they have done something wonderful or have really messed up and had to repent we tell them we still love them and always will love them. We must praise them and tell them we are proud of them for having the courage to repent. This is a moment where we as parents have a chance to break the condemnation that the enemy, the devil, wants our children to live in. They need to see the forgiveness of God walked out in our actions. I wish I could tell you that I did this perfectly and as a result my children never struggled with condemnation but like a lot of the things, Jerry and I have put in this book what we learned from God as He corrected our failures. My hope is that you can learn from our stories and not repeat some of our blunders.

Now I want to switch the dialogue and talk about positive, intentional ways to celebrate your children. If you have never read the book *The Five Love Languages* by Gary Chapman, I recommend it. In brief, individuals express love in one of these five ways: acts of service, gifts giving, words of affirmation, touch, and quality time. I bring this up because one of my love languages is gift giving. I love to give gifts! So, for me some really important times to celebrate my children are birthdays and any other gift-giving holiday.

I especially believe a birthday should be really special. After all, it is custom made for singling your child out and saying, "No one is as uniquely amazing as you!" So, in the Burbee house birthdays have always been special. I believe you can be very creative on birthdays without spending a lot of money. Here are some of our birthday blowouts. For our daughter, we did dress up tea parties or homemade spa days with her friends. For our boys, we had a pirate birthday where everyone had to dress and talk like a pirate. We even had fake gold coin treasure hunts to find the presents. But, I will tell you, two of our favorites were because of having summer birthdays. One was a huge squirt gun war all over the yard. My husband and son's favorite started out as a wiffle ball game on a watered-down yard that turned into an all out mudslide with wrestling. Now, I know to some people the idea of hosing down your yard and having twelve to twenty little boys and their dads (the dads couldn't resist) sliding in the mud is not something you'd consider. However, I was not that into making sure my house looked perfect and knew my son's memories of a blowout birthday would last longer than it took my yard to recover from the adventure. I'm sure these examples will help you create some of your own fun times to celebrate your children.

I must preface that the celebration has to be appropriate for the child and their age. I have heard of parents spending tons of money on very inappropriate parties for their children. Your one-year-old doesn't need a trip to Disney World. That would be inappropriate. Throwing money at a child does not say "You are special," and an extravagant birthday doesn't make up for months of ignoring them. You see, I believe the child remembers mommy dressed like a pirate or covered in mud far more than Disney World. Find out what your children love, then make them feel special by using it to celebrate them.

When my kids got older and we had a little more money, things changed. For instance, we took a few trips to St Louis and Kansas City (each are about a three-hour drive away) to attend a professional ball game. We took a trip to an art museum. I think, though, the group of boys running around the basement in the dark having a dart gun war probably ranks higher in my son's favorite parties. Sometimes now my kids all want to gather at our house for games and a special meal. The point is I always try to make birthdays special. This year I hung up a big "Happy Birthday" banner for my twenty-two-year-old son because he wanted to gather and watch the football game for his birthday. These times are made more special because I celebrate my children every day to make sure they always understand how valuable they are.

Other ways to celebrate children are little things, like love letters for Valentine's day, lunch box notes or, sending balloons or flowers to school or work. But nothing ranks higher than being there for them. When my kids played sports, I would be the loudest, proudest mom there. I have framed and hung their high school art work on my walls. The most important thing to me is making sure my children know I think they are extraordinary. Look at your child and see what they like, then make sure they know it is important to you too because it is important to them.

Each child is unique and speaks their own love language. If you pay attention, your child will reveal what they enjoy and need from you. I did special, unique things for each child. I had pet names or phrases I only used for each one. For my son Michael ,the phrase "Budapest" has a special meaning between us. (If you want to know what it means, you will have to ask him.) Joe was my "hold hands" child or "tickle me on the floor, Daddy!" Amy really loved a drive to window shop and talk (actually so she could talk) which I enjoyed more than I can express. She also loved reading a special book together before bed. Fit what you do to what is special for your children, and it needs to be as different for each child as they are.

Find out what makes your child tick. Our Daddy God is often called the Lover of our Soul, and our soul is what makes us unique. These are those things I love to do or things I am passionate about. God doesn't cookie cut us, or the way He loves us. I am always amazed at how different God speaks to me versus how He speaks to my husband. I shouldn't be though because God knows me uniquely. He even knows exactly how to discipline me which probably differs from how He disciplines you. This leads to my next point: celebrating your child in a way that speaks to who they are means you have to slow down and spend time listening and getting to know your child. Nothing is sadder than giving a Barbie to a little girl who wants a book (except maybe forgetting her birthday all together). You do have to spend time with them one-on-one. You don't always have to take a vacation day from work to spend it with your child. Sometimes it can just be fifteen to thirty minutes a day, having a conversation, or special bedtime ritual; anything to make sure the child knows you care.

I've said this before and I know I'll say it again, your children are your number one disciples. Don't let the devil lull you into the daily grind and business of life so much that you forget what is truly important. If my children do not make it into eternity with God, I am pretty sure the rest of that stuff won't matter. I have friends whose adult children are not saved and their anguish is palpable. That is a grief I am not sure I could bear.

Let me say it again. Our children have to know they are uniquely loved by you and by God. For me, my children are beyond a doubt some of the most precious relationships in my life. I could brag forever on how extremely amazing I think each of them are. I know I have never regretted any sacrifice we ever made for our children. Every conversation or moment of play spent with them when they were young opened the way to continue talking as they moved into their teen years. When we celebrate our children for who God made them, we are bringing glory to God.

JERRY

Celebrating your child can take many forms, but at its core, it means demonstrating sincere excitement. This excitement can be expressed in how you respect their autonomy, recognizing their uniqueness and specialness, or through a vibrant appreciation that they are in your life. This type of celebration cannot begin until you know your child. You cannot know your child unless you have spent time with them. That time must be a balanced mixture of them learning from you and you learning from them. A much appreciated grace that God granted me was the desire to experience the world from my child's perspective. At every stage and through every phase, I wanted to know what they were thinking and how they were feeling. I wanted to learn from them. Keeping a child-like heart in the adult world can be challenging. I enjoyed immersing myself in a child's world to be reminded of the simple beauty of God's world. Occasionally, information was collected through direct questioning, but the best insight I gained was when I allowed them to direct me through their world. At times, we would do activities I directed, and through observation, I learned some of their likes, dislikes, strengths, weaknesses, etc. But the grandest adventure occurred when I let them direct the activity. I wasn't the boss or the one who determined how things were to play out. I would occasionally have to "step out of character" and enforce Dad's rules of appropriate behavior, but for the most part, I went on their adventure. We played the game they wanted to play, even if the rules were different than the ones that came in the box. Or, I would create a game, and together, we would make up the rules as we went along. My way of celebrating them was to respect them as an equal and to join them in a frolic through imagination.

"Wait! Won't there be confusion about who is in charge? Are you not encouraging your child to boss you around and create confusion concerning the parent-child boundaries?"

No.

I felt that because they knew I was humble enough to enter their world and to celebrate their uniqueness, I gained the respect to correct them in a manner that would build them up and not tear them down. I see the role of the parent to be one that emulates how God has interacted with us. Philippians 2 describes how Jesus left the glory of heaven and took on the role of a servant. He humbled Himself so He could engage with us on our level. To become a child in the presence of my children gave me the opportunity to experience the world together with them. In this world I entered, I was able to demonstrate the character and nature their father wanted from his children similar to the way Jesus came and demonstrated how His Father wanted His children to live. Those who knew the Father had no difficulty seeing the Son for who He was. Those who did not accept the Son as a

35

representative of the Father had the opportunity for Him to clarify the misunderstandings. If, while we were playing this way, my child demonstrated arrogance, disrespect, or grumbling, it gave me the chance to ask a question, correct directly, or tell a story. Jesus turned over tables in the Temple, asked the woman at the well a lot of questions, told parables, encouraged, corrected, and loved those He encountered. Having an opportunity for the Father to come into my world and frolic with me through communion with his Son, what is a better celebration of how He values me?

I wanted each of my children to know they were someone to be celebrated. Debbie is the queen of Christmas, birthdays, and public displays of affection. I was not easily inclined to celebrate them in her manner. I learned much from her and enjoyed watching the light on my kids' faces as she celebrated them. However, I tended to celebrate in one-on-one situations. I developed in my ability to celebrate them openly, joining Debbie in yelling for them at their games or clapping wildly during their performances. Yet I wanted those demonstrations to be more than facades of praise. If I had not taken the effort to step into their world, it would have been difficult to applaud the things that were important to them. Being in their world, seeing their priorities and passions, gave me insight on how to celebrate them as individuals. I wanted each of them to know they were important to me, that I valued them, and that I was excited about them. They needed to know they were more exciting than a football game on TV or more important than some project I was tinkering with. I wanted them to see I chose them. I could have done something else, but I wanted to enter into their world and see what was important to them. Ten or fifteen minutes in the Lego closet with Michael (a small closet in his room where we kept all the Legos), giving him the opportunity to show me what he and his friends had been building and the significance of all the particulars of each build gave me a chance to see him as he was:

"This piece is on there so when the plane flies over, you have a gun to shoot them down. Andrew thought this piece fit better here but I wanted it over here, so he built his own and I built one for myself."

"Why did you only put three wheels on it, instead of four?"

"Well, I could only find three wheels that matched, but it moves better like this."

"Yeah, you're right. I like that. That's pretty cool."

One fall day at Grandma's house, I was able to join Joseph and "Johnny Red" as they planned an attack against the bad guys:

"Dad, you have to crawl over there on your stomach and I'll stay here behind the bush. When Johnny Red gives the signal, we'll charge the wall."

"Who's Johnny Red?"

"He's the guy over there who is leading this bunch. He wants to get those bad guys."

"Ok. Do I have a gun, or a stick, or something when we charge the wall?"

"Oh, yeah. You have a flash gun and me and Johnny have bolt pistols."

"What's a flash gun? And a bolt pistol?"

"You know. You pull the trigger and 'Flash' the gun shoots. Mine has the bolt on top that moves back and forth."

"Alright. Let me know when Johnny gives the signal in case I don't hear him."

With Amy I learned many things about appropriate Polly Pocket etiquette:

"No, Dad, that one goes over there and this one goes here."

"Does she need to go to bed? Or is she supposed to be fixing supper?"

"Silly Daddy, it's not even dark outside, why would she be going to bed now?"

"You're right. How silly of me."

To me, these stories, and countless others, are the celebration of our togetherness and my celebration of their wonderfulness.

Parenting is about shaping and leading. When our children hear us cheering from the crowd or when we join them in their inner world, they know they are important to us. You have permission to guide them, to cheer for them, to play with them, to correct them, and to celebrate them the way the Father celebrates us. "The Lord your God is with you, the Mighty Warrior who saves. He will take great delight in you; in his love he will no longer rebuke you, but will rejoice over you with singing" (Zeph. 3:17 NIV).

DEBBIE'S ADDENDUM

As my husband and I were reading through this chapter again, I sensed in my spirit that some of you dads were thinking "Well that's all well and good for him, but I'm really busy. I work hard." I felt like I needed to add that during the time our children were little, Jerry was in medical school, internship, and residency. It was normal during these days for him to work eighty plus hour weeks, but when he walked through our door, our children were priority for him. He never sat in his chair watching TV. No, he played with the kids. Each of the stories you just read were in some of the busiest times of both of our lives. It does not matter how busy we are, our children need to know they are still important. Make the most of every moment you do have with them and find a way to make it count. You can do this.

CHAPTER 5
SETTING YOUR CHILD UP FOR FAILURE

DEBBIE

Walk with me through a couple of situations and be really honest about what you think. Imagine you finally get that date night out with your spouse and the restaurant sets you next to a family with three kids. One is tied in a high chair and can't move around, but the other two are running around the table, yelling and chasing each other while the exasperated mother keeps pleading with them to sit down. Meanwhile, the one in the high chair is throwing food and banging the table. You get the picture. Now, do you walk away wanting to be friends with that family and grateful they went out to eat to share their joyful family with the world? What about the kid at soccer practice who keeps pushing your child down, and his or her mommy is almost afraid to do anything? I could go on, but you probably get the picture. When we come across children who do not obey their parents, we don't really like them. If we are honest, some of you probably know families you don't want to spend time with because of the way the children behave. They are even the children other children don't like.

The problem in these instances is that the child is bearing the consequences that should go to the parent. When we do not discipline our children, we set them up to fail. Now, I am sure when you decided to have children, one of your goals was to raise them to be successful in life. I am also sure that most parents who do not discipline their children have a lot of different reasons for doing that, but watching their child become the neighborhood monster is not one of them.

I have exaggerated a little here to make a point (but really not too much). The Bible says in Proverbs 13:24 NIV, "Whoever spares the rod hates their children, but the one who loves their children is careful to discipline them." We like to quote this verse as "spare the rod and spoil the child," but that is not what the passage says. It says, "If I spare the rod, I hate my child." I would go so far as to say that we set them up for others to hate them too. When we don't discipline our children, we allow them to live in a state of rebellion. In 1 Samuel 15, Samuel informs King Saul that God is going to rip his kingdom from his hands. Now, my take on King Saul was that he was a man who was used to doing whatever he wanted and always getting his way. Maybe he was that really cute kid who could get away with anything because he would give that cute, dimpled smile and his mommy would just crumble. I don't know, but he did seem to think he could do whatever he wanted for the moment and later offer a little sacrifice so that God would be okay with it. If we start in 1 Samuel 15:22, "Samuel replied: 'Does the Lord delight in burnt offerings and sacrifices as much as in obeying the Lord? To obey is better than sacrifice, and to heed is better than the fat of rams.'" Then in verse 23, Samuel says, "For rebellion is like the sin of divination, and arrogance like the evil of idolatry." Did you hear that? Rebellion is like divination. Divination is witchcraft. So, when you look at it, when you allow your child to rebel, or be rebellious toward you, you are letting them participate in the sin of witchcraft and idolatry. It is no wonder the Bible says the person who does not discipline their child hates them.

It used to baffle me sometimes to read verses like Numbers 14:18 where the Bible says God punishes the children for the sins of the parents to the third and fourth generation. When we look at this situation, it truly is the parent's sin which has led the child down a path of destruction. Ephesians 6:12 and Colossians 3:20 are two scriptures that tell children to obey their parents. Ephesians 6:12 specifically states, "Children, obey your parents in the Lord, for this is right. Honor your father and mother—which is the first commandment with a promise—so that it may go well with you and that you may enjoy a long life on the earth." We are the ones who teach our children how to obey. We must show them that disobedience or rebellion always has a consequence. My children learned very quickly that if mommy or daddy said to stop something, we meant it, and not obeying meant some form of punishment always. As they grew older, sometimes all it would take was to give them "the look." (Every mom knows what I am talking about: the serious facial expression with eyebrows raised and direct eye contact. That look still lets my sons know to toe the line)

Children will always test you, and I know it isn't always convenient to follow through, but my children had to learn that no place was a safe place for disobedience. If my child threw a fit in Walmart, I would leave my cart right where it was and we would head to the car for a spanking. After they had been dealt with, then I returned to finish my shopping. When we are busy trying to take care of the needs of our family, moms sometimes it feels like, "What would it hurt to just let this go?" One of our friends, who had a very strong-willed daughter, used to tell the story of her child laying on the floor in Walmart, throwing a fit, and her having her foot over child's back while she wrote her check at the cashier. I laughed really hard when my friend told this story, but one day I was in the post office having a similar confrontation with my own child and realized I was headed in the same direction if I didn't change. My daughter had kicked off her shoe and we were doing battle as I tried to put it back on. A sweet, little old lady tried to distract her from the battle so I could get her shoe on. I don't know if it was the embarrassment in that lady's eyes or the looks on the faces of the one's trying to avoid us that made things click for me. I do know I made the decision that her little world of control was going to change. That is when I realized trying to ignore situations, instead of dealing with them, was not working. Believe me, when your child knows you will scoop them up and head for the car to deal with their rebellion, things begin to change. My priority had to be my daughter.

I remember the first time my toddler boys tried to throw themselves on the floor in a fit. I'll never forget the look on their faces when my husband scooped them up, held them at eye level, and firmly said, "You will never do that again, son." Believe me, they both tried it once and never again. Now dads, I will tell you this is just as much your responsibility as it is mom's. Remember, they are your children too. If you see your child challenging mom, you need to step in and put an end to that right there. When you do nothing, you are giving your child permission to dishonor their mother by the very act of dishonoring her yourself.

I remember telling Jerry when we had our sons that it would not take long before the boys were bigger than me, and if he did not show them that to disobey mom meant consequences from him, then I would be in trouble. One day, my boys reached the point when they decided mommy couldn't spank hard, so they didn't have to obey me. I told Jerry when he got home that night and he promptly marched my boys to his shop, and together they cut out a paddle from a piece of particle board, covered it with duct tape, then drilled holes in it. They brought the paddle to me and Jerry made sure when I used it that first time that they felt it. We dubbed the paddle "Mr. Silver." The funny thing is I don't remember having to use Mr. Silver again because for my boys just knowing I would was all it took. I guess it made a strong enough impression on them that they told their friends, who told their parents, because we got a couple of calls from friends requesting their own. The need for obedience was made even stronger in my boys when Jerry made them help make a Mr. Silver for their friends.

Since I mentioned spanking as discipline, I want to take a moment to discuss it as appropriate discipline. We reserved spanking for rebellion that was willful and conscious disobedience, not for youthful mistakes. Spanking is done on the fleshy part of the bottom, over clothes, and should never leave a mark. I do not believe in ever abusing or breaking a child's spirit. I will also point out that you can wound with words sometimes more than you can with a paddle. Always remember your child is first and foremost God's child, so treat them as such. NEVER discipline out of anger. Discipline is for training, not to be done out of frustration. After we disciplined our children, we would hold them and reassure them of our love. This moment is usually our best teachable moment, so be sure the child understands why it happened, and now that the consequence for their action is done, let them know you still love them and it is finished.

Now let me talk about parents who let their children be in control of a room. These are children who have been taught that they are the center of the universe and everything should revolve around them. Now, don't get me wrong, my children knew they were some of the most important people in the world to me, but they also needed to know how to be polite and behave in public. Constantly interrupting mommy and daddy so that it prevents them from having a conversation is not showing honor. Just as our children must be taught not to disobey, which brings dishonor, they also need to be taught how to bring honor.

My parents have a little dog that is my mom's constant companion. That dog has been taught that she rules the house. When someone comes to visit my parents, the little dog gets so excited. She is sure everyone who walks through the door is there to see her and to pet her. She jumps up on them or the chair and won't even let them talk to my parents until she feels she has gotten sufficient recognition. My mom will even scold us if we don't pay enough attention to the dog first. The problem comes when the visitor is not family and they are not coming to see the dog. I know my example here is a dog, but sadly the same is true for the way a lot of parents let their children behave when company comes.

Whenever a group of people gather together, your child does not need to be the center of attention. Most people do not come to your house to watch your children demand all of the room's attention. Teach them to not interrupt. Teach them to self-entertain appropriately for their age. Teach them to play quietly, or as they get older, teach them how to listen respectfully. Children can, and need, to be involved in God conversations in your home. My children joined the prayers we prayed for people in our home. We had some intense God moments where our adult worship ended with my children on their faces crying out to

Jesus. My children would sometimes prophesy over our guests. These moments would never have happened if every time we had company my children demanded all the attention. Children learn how to honor and give respect to others, just as they learn how to obey.

God makes promises to children who honor their parents, that being it may go well with them and they will enjoy a long life. I want these promises for my children. Having children is such a blessing. That blessing comes with the responsibility to train the child. It is never too late to show or instruct your child that disobedience has consequences. My personal experience is that it is easier to teach this to children at an early age. I saw the fruit of this with my own children. My husband could scoop up a screaming toddler and make a point. If you haven't made this point by the time they are teens, you have allowed rebellion to rule in their hearts for a long time. It will take work to retrain them. It is so important that you take the time when they are younger to instill both obedience and honorinto them.

A child who disobeys their parents and dishonors them rarely does anything different with God. Isaiah 30:9 talks about how the Israelites were a rebellious people. It goes on to say they had deceitful children who were unwilling to listen to the Lord's instruction. First Peter 3:12 says, "The eyes of the Lord are on the righteous and His ears are attentive to their prayer, but the face of the Lord is against those who do evil." Second Timothy 3 talks about how in the end times people will be disobedient to parents. These scriptures put the fear of God in me. I do not want to be the reason the face of the Lord is against my child. Remember, the Bible says if I don't discipline my child, I hate them. God knows best, my friend. Over and over, man has messed up because we think we know better than God and His word. God's Word is true today and will be true through eternity.

My children did not rebel as teenagers. In fact, we had an amazing house full of children who loved us and loved God. We do not by any chance take credit for this. Tt was all God. I will say, however, that we were obedient to His word. We disciplined our children, but more importantly, we trained them. It is possible for your children to fall in love with God at a young age and become real disciples. They are, however, born with a sin nature that if allowed to grow and fester can derail everything. Your children are worth whatever effort it takes to love them biblically. Loving them biblically means disciplining them. Remember, the second part of Proverbs 13:24 says, "The one who loves their children is careful to discipline them." Amen.

JERRY

In raising our children, a primary requirement for me was that they had been taught to respect God and others. Our continual goal for them is to love God with all their heart, soul, mind, and strength and to love their neighbor as themselves. Love has many expressions that are summarized by Philippians 2:3-4: "Do nothing out of selfish ambition or vain conceit. Rather, in humility value others above yourselves, not looking to your own interests but each of you to the interests of the others" (NIV). This is how we humans can emulate the love of Christ. Since the flesh has no difficulty demanding its desires, disciplining our children focuses on teaching them to know when and how to restrain those desires and how to honor others.

The house we lived in when the kids were small had a decent-sized backyard where they could play. For their safety, one of the things I did was to point out the boundaries and some rules for playing in the yard. On the north side was the house. "Don't throw things at the house." On the west side was our neighbor's tall wooden fence. "The neighbors have a dog on the other side of the fence. It is not a good idea to stand at the fence and agitate the dog. The neighbors won't appreciate that." On the south side, the edge of our yard had some small trees and bushes that separated it from our neighbor's yard. They put a lot of effort into caring for their flowers and bushes. "You are not to go into the neighbor's yard unless you are retrieving a wayward toy. When you do go over there, be careful not to trample on their flowers. That is bad." On the east side, we had a picket fence that separated the yard from the street. Traffic on that street was minimal, but we lived on a corner and frequently cars zoomed around the corner unexpectedly. "DO NOT GO OUT INTO THE STREET TO GET YOUR BALL. If your ball goes out of the yard, come get me and I will get it."

While out in the yard with them (or as I spied on them through the dining room window), I would watch and see how they obeyed these simple rules. Playing ball nearly always resulted in one bouncing in the wrong direction. Occasionally, one would bang against the house, but usually not intentionally, and I would simply have to remind them to be careful. The next one landed in the neighbor's flowers. "Be careful. Don't crush anything." After a few times of demonstrating what I meant, they were able to retrieve the errant ball without damage to the foliage. On the west side, we never had much of a problem. The fence was too high for the ball to go over regularly, and they did not have interest in the dog. That boundary was rarely breached, and therefore, required minimal correction. The big problem was the street. In the heat of a game, sometimes small boys forget what they have been told. The house and the flowers were replaceable, but a car versus a small boy would not be as forgiving. This rule required more diligence on my part. If something hit the house or if they were a little rough on the flowers, I could briefly say something then let play continue. If the ball went into the street, I could not be lenient on their disobedience. The potential for serious harm was too great. As they got older, I taught them how to watch for traffic and how to retrieve their ball safely, but only after they learned to obey the rule without exception.

This illustration is to show how I view discipline. My goal is to teach my children the boundaries, how and why to respect those boundaries, and eventually, teach them how to navigate encounters with them. Every boundary must be prayerfully considered, have a predetermined punishment for disobedience, both you and your spouse must be in agreement on the boundary and the punishment, and the rules need to be consistently enforced. Unfortunately, it is not quite that simple, but it gets us pointed in the right direction. The reality of our world is that some rules are non-negotiable. Excuses and sympathy can sometimes be a consideration in a response to wanton activity, but that cannot be expected. Disobedience leads to death. In the case of the illustration, a car could have killed one of my children. In matters of the kingdom, disobedience harms our relationship with God, and if repentance is not embraced, permanent separation from God, i.e., spiritual death, is likely. Demanding that a child obey is for their good. Grace and mercy are necessary, for that is how God loves us, but continued, unrepentant disobedience is not to be tolerated. We have to teach our children this reality. We have to demonstrate it. We have to enforce it. To not do so sets your child up for failure. It means you hate your children and you're selfish. It's that serious.

One of the things I learned from a friend of ours, Tracy Pingel, was to teach our children that there are places to go wild and there are places where you have to sit still. As a parent, think through carefully how you designate situations and then be consistent. We developed an informal classification system to help the kids know what was appropriate. "In this place you act like you would at Grandma's house." "While we are here, you can play like you do when we go to the park." "This is a place with lots of strangers, so do not wander off; stay close to me or Mom." Be sure to be specific in these designations. "At Grandma's you cannot run in the house. No playing with balls, except outside. No loud yelling or talking." "At this park you can go anywhere between here and that fence. Don't go on the merry-go-round unless I am with you." As we were arriving at a place, we usually had a brief discussion in the car about their expected behavior. We either explained what we wanted from them or reminded them of what the rules were last time. We also explained the punishment for disobedience. Then, we had to enforce it. I had no problem saying to my host, "Excuse me, I need to tend to my child. My son knows he is not supposed to be jumping on your couch, and he and I need to have a discussion about his behavior." Even if the host was gracious and said, "Oh, don't worry about it. It's an old couch." I would politely thank him for his graciousness but would still excuse myself to correct my son. I wanted to demonstrate that I respected the situation and the people and wanted to help my kids develop that ability. Their behavior was my responsibility, not because I did not want to be embarrassed, but because my children needed to learn respect. Fathers, we must engage in this role. This is on you. I have difficulty thinking of anything I would not interrupt in order to protect my child from the damage that can come to them because I did not make them accountable to the rules. Children definitely need to know about grace and mercy, but they first have to understand the importance of obedience. This does not mean I am harsh or unloving. With respect and tenderness, firm application of discipline and punishment can be wrought upon the young soul that has been wayward. My mindset was that I would do whatever was necessary, short of emotional or physical abuse, in order to teach my child the importance of obedience.

Questions that parents need to ask themselves:

- Have I considered what is appropriate behavior for my children in different situations?
- Do I allow my child to behave as they choose or do I set boundaries?
- Have I considered how my child's behavior is impacting others?
- What are the appropriate behaviors for: Walmart, church, a friend's house, the park, etc.?

As you consider these questions, please invite the input of others. The pirouette your daughter is doing in the middle of the room may be cute to you, but may not be appreciated by the others who are trying to have a serious conversation. You may think you are letting your child feel the unhindered presence of God as they run around the sanctuary after church, but the three people they have run into may not agree. Teaching them to be respectful and considerate of others begins with us parents being considerate and respectful of others. My biggest failure was, even though I instructed them in appropriate behavior, sometimes I demonstrated disrespect and they mirrored my actions. The consistency between our instructions and our actions reinforce or destroy what we are trying to teach them about respect.

Success in the kingdom is contingent on loving God and loving others ["Love the Lord your God with all your heart and with all your soul and with all your strength and with all your mind"; and, "Love your neighbor as yourself" (Luke 10:27 NIV).] Loving God involves obedience ["Jesus replied, 'Anyone who loves me will obey my teaching. My Father will love them, and we will come to them and make our home with them'" (John 14:23 NIV).] If we do not instill a love for God through obedience, we set our children up to fail. If we are not consistent with our standards, we can frustrate them and create confusion.

By now you have realized there are very few things in parenting that are rock solid absolutes. Even those things that are absolute are not very specific, like love your child, care for your child, encourage your child. These last two chapters emphasize the two extremes that parents have to learn to balance. Celebrating your child and making them feel special is an absolute. Disciplining your child so that they are respectful while teaching them self-control is also an absolute.

CHAPTER 6

BE A PARENT, NOT A FRIEND

DEBBIE

Hollywood is always making movies about young girls having babies because they are longing for someone to love them. To me that is a tragic scenario. That little baby cannot give you identity and security. I bring this up because some of the new parenting models out there today are, well, just flat out wacky, putting expectations on children that are impossible for their little abilities to perform. There is one model called free range parenting where you basically let the child call the shots. I've heard some European countries are talking about not even assigning a sex to your child until they are three and then letting them choose if they want to identify as a male or female. In my mind, this is pure lunacy. What other major life decisions do we leave to three-year-olds? Next, will we let them vote or go to war at four? Now, I may step on some toes here but God is the one who assigns our sex. If I am born with an XX chromosome pair, I am a girl. If I have an XY pair, I am male. I may be a girl that likes hunting and sports, but I am still female. The point is children do not know what is best for themselves and letting them rule the house is crazy! They need a parent.

Another problem I see is the parent who is so insecure that their child won't "like" them that they are afraid to parent. To me the root of this lunacy starts from adults having no identity and being so insecure because they don't understand who God made them to be and what He says about them. They seek validation from their kids in place of that. Value comes from God and God alone. Your value comes not from what you do but in the fact that you are God's child.

Children are the ones who should crave security. They are born helpless into this world, dependent on their parents for everything. The other day I was holding a friend's fussy newborn and I realized he kept showing a startle reflex, so I wrapped him up real tight in a swaddle blanket. You guessed it, he settled down and stopped fussing. See, even newborns need to feel secure boundaries.

Children are given to us to love and care for. It is our job to be their parent. We are to train them as Proverbs 22:6 says, " Train up a child in the way he should go and when he is old he will not depart from it." They are not able to tell us what to do to raise them. In fact, when you make the decision to have a child, you are saying you are ready to lay your life down for the welfare of another. You have forfeited your right to privacy, sleep, and even sometimes meeting your own needs or desires. You are saying for however long it takes to ensure this child has a successful life, you will lay down your own life to ensure that happens. No sleeping in on your day off. No more spending that extra cash on a new dress or hairstyle. Sometimes you will find you are excited if you get to shower that day. Parenting is not for cowards. In fact, my own children will tell you I have said many times that if someone is too selfish to give up their own life for another, they have no right to bring a child into this world.

I don't mean to sound harsh but that child did not ask to be born. You are the one who brought him into this world. Now that you have it is your responsibility to parent.

When our daughter was three, we began to have problems with her wanting to rule the house or boss me around. She would throw a fit if I didn't pick out the exact outfit she wanted to wear. She would only eat macaroni and cheese, green beans, and peaches. One day, we were driving down the road and she was in her car seat kicking her feet and punching the air yelling, "You stop this car, Mommy! You stop this car right now!" Fortunately, we had an older couple we trusted and they advised us that we were giving her too many choices.

Well, I am the type of person who usually has thought through my actions and have a reason for what I am doing. I prefer to understand the reasoning behind something before I just change what I am doing. In this case, my parents had followed the dictator style of parenting and as a result, I felt like it was hard for me to make my own choices sometimes. I wanted my child to know her own preferences, but I prayed and asked, "God, what to do for my child?" As always, God answered. I was listening to a radio program and Dr. James Dobson, a noted family expert, came on. Dr. Dobson began to talk about children and the choices we give them. You can bet at this point I began to really pay attention. He began to describe my daughter's actions to a tee. The summary of what he said was that we let our children make choices that are not important, like what color glass to drink from or which pajamas to wear to bed, but our children do not know the difference between an unimportant decision and an important one. From this they then begin to believe they are in charge and can make all the rules. He continued to say this causes them to feel insecure and they begin to act out, saying things like, "No, Mommy, you go to bed," after being told what to do. Dr. Dobson basically said that until a child is old enough to not care if they make a decision, they are not ready to be offered choices. So we began to take away our daughter's choices. At first, it was World War III. She even asked my mom on the phone when she was coming to visit because she "had lots of problems." The amazing part of this story was that after that initial battle we had a new child. She was happy. She had a parent making her choices and taking care of things so she felt secure and able to just enjoy being a child. We also realized that anytime she started acting out again we had slipped up and started giving her choices again.

Children need us to be parents. They want to know where their boundaries are. One of the worst things I see parents do is move the boundaries on their children. How do they do that, you ask? Well, the parent tells their child to do something, like sit down or you will be punished, and when the child disobeys, the parent just repeats what she said. Finally, the parent just explodes because the child hasn't obeyed. Well, why should they obey when your words mean nothing? When you do this, the child will keep pushing to find out where the boundaries really are. If you tell your child to do something, they need to know you will only tell them once and if they disobey there will be consequences. The Bible says in Matthew 5:37 that our yes should be yes, meaning basically our words need to be true and if we say something we should mean it. Firm boundaries make for secure children.

If I am so afraid that my child will be mad at me that I cannot be the adult and put their needs first, then I am demonstrating what the Bible talks about when it says not to provoke your child to wrath. Parenting is about helping your child grow up to be successful in their life, and that takes making the tough decisions, not the popular ones. When you don't make your child mind you, he or she stops listening and eventually you as the parent end up mad all the time. You are creating the very thing you fear by not parenting because children who grow up with wimpy parents do not grow up to respect them.

In case no one has ever told you this, I will: you have permission to parent. I will say it again: you have permission to parent. Be the adult. Make the hard decisions and fight for your child's success. I've heard so many parents say, "I would die for my child." Now, I'm not doubting that, and since it is very unlikely that situation will arise, we won't really know. To me, the true test is "Will you die to yourself and make the important decisions for your child's success?"

The other day, I was talking to a mom of a teenage son who was in a bad place. As a young boy, he had been on fire for Jesus, but now he was telling his parents that he was not even sure he even believed in God. As we discussed it further, she said that when he went to high school he started hanging out with a new group of friends. They fancied themselves as intellectuals and could just not embrace the Bible as truth. Then she said they were also exploring the idea of their sexuality, and several of those boys were thinking they might be homosexual. At this point, I replied that the first thing I would do was to get him away from these so-called friends. Her reply was that they were his friends from the public school, so she couldn't do anything about that. I know people think I sound pretty radical at times, but if he were my child, nothing would be more important than saving him. My job, his schooling, him being angry—nothing! If it took me quitting my job to take him out of public school and start homeschooling him, I would immediately. Those friends would no longer be his main influence. If I lost my son, I guarantee none of this other stuff would be very important. So, in reality, you will probably never be in a situation where you would have to die for your child, but most of us (no, all of us) will face situations where we will have to choose whether to die to ourselves for our child.

I can tell you that all three of our children have grown up to be our friends. In fact, they are some of our closest friends, but that was not the goal. The goal was to be the parent they needed. A parent who set firm boundaries because we love them. A parent who meant what was said and expected to be obeyed. In fact, I learned early on not to flippantly say "no" to my child's request because if that child challenged me, I had to win that battle. Winning the battle was so much easier if I had a reason for saying "no" in the first place.

As parents, our job is to train our children, protect them, be their covering, and meet their needs. Nowhere does this include being their friend so they can meet some need in me. Get your needs met by God and the godly men and women He has put you with. Then, be the parent your child deserves.

JERRY

I think the attraction to becoming a friend versus stepping up to parent is that the weight of the relationship is borne by the parent. A friend is not responsible for a friend. We can be concerned and offer advice, but if they ignore it, it's not our problem. With friendships, we can engage as desired, whereas a parent has a child 24/7 and is tethered to them regardless of whatever else may be occurring. But who better to carry the weight of a flowering relationship than the one who has been given the grace to carry it? That grace is supernatural power from God to accomplish what we could not have done for ourselves. You are that person, and you have that grace. Admittedly, one of my parenting goals was that when my children became adults, we would be friends. But even then, I am still their dad.

I also think sometimes we have memories of our own parents being harsh and uninformed when they corrected us. We wish our parents had taken the time to experience our world and walk with us rather than interfere and restrict our dreams. Therefore, we want our children to feel respected and trusted to make choices without judgmental assumptions of their inadequacy. We may think the goal of parenting is that they have permission to express their autonomy without domineering lordship from out-of-touch old fogeys. These are admirable goals, but reaching these goals come from embracing parenting, not abandoning it.

The best relationships are built on love and honor. When you were wanting your parents to experience your world, you were wanting to be honored and loved. And that's what you want for your child, for them to feel loved and honored. You want them to see, feel, and know love so they can recognize the authentic and reject all counterfeits. Though our modern culture displays honor as a reward for achievements and love as an expression of feelings, those are shallow definitions. Love and honor stem from a personal conviction to treat others according to the recognition and appreciation of their value. This conviction is born from having embraced the importance of these foundations in our own lives and the realization that this is how God treats us. Honor reveals an estimation of value. It is not simply the value of people's actions; it is the value of their humanity. Honor instigates actions that always respect uniqueness and autonomy. Love is honoring the person by giving the best you have for their good. Love and honor together generate a gift you give to another person, regardless of their response. I choose to treat everyone this way, even if I don't feel like it and they don't enjoy it. When I recognize that my child is fresh meat for a wolfish world, I honor and love my child by protecting them from the wolves until I have had time to train them to protect themselves. I honor my child by making the effort to teach them from my experiences, unveiling my weakness and my strengths, displaying the humility of one who has had successes and failures. To burden them with choices when they have not been trained is like giving them a tricycle for a demolition derby. That is not love. With an expectation of growth, we respectfully correct and discipline, even when it is not appreciated.

Men, honor and love starts[9] with you. How you treat your wife, your children, your friends, your coworkers, and the strangers on the street set the definitions of these concepts in your children. They hear your words and see your life. They absorb the contradictions between what you say and how you act. These contradictions, if uncorrected, will bring distortion to their ability to hear God and to live a life of love. They notice if you honor all people. They watch to see if you love your wife like Christ loves the Church by laying down your life for hers. Do you love God with your whole heart, soul, mind, and strength? Do you love your neighbor as yourself? Remember, you set the standard for your home. The modern father is depicted as the lazy guy who tries to be his kids' buddy and leaves all the parenting to the mother. Gentlemen, if you are sitting back and watching your three-year-old throw a fit and are wondering why your wife isn't doing something about it, get off your butt and be a man.

Stand up and take your place as the shepherd of your family. When the wolves come, when the sheep wander off, when they need fresh water, when they need to be led to a safe place, you are that shepherding man. Correction begins with us. Don't leave it for your wife. Stop looking the other way. If you want to provoke our children to anger, don't discipline them and don't instruct them in the ways of the Lord. It is important to father. Being a soft, ambiguous presence in your children's lives might seem to make them like us more, but we harm them when we do not love as the Father loves. Ephesians 6:4 was addressed to us: "Fathers, do not provoke your children to anger, but bring them up in the discipline and instruction of the Lord" (ESV). You will feel inadequate, overwhelmed, or unappreciated, but you cannot let that lure you into the trap which seeks to please your children through a shallow relationship rather than engaging them in the fullness of love. Growth as an individual will probably be necessary, but that is what grace is all about. If you're having trouble, acknowledge your sin, repent, pray for God's intervention, and then follow the guidance of the Holy Spirit.

Being rejected by our children is probably one of the more painful things a parent experiences, yet God's response was to humble Himself, take on the role of a servant, set the standard for behavior, sacrifice as needed, and correct when needed with occasional judgment. Through this response, He demonstrates the fullness of His nature—love. We can parent, and we can love like God does. Striving primarily to have our children as friends, though pleasing in the short-term, will have unwanted long-term consequences.

This humbling might require a couple of nights on your knees crying out to God. It will definitely demand cutting off dead works of the flesh, amputation of selfish desires, and repositioning yourself. I would suggest you ask God to send a father in the faith who can train you so you can train your children. Remember, parent comes first, friend second.

CHAPTER 7

KNOW WHAT YOUR CHILD IS TAUGHT

DEBBIE

Across the world today, most governments have some form of educational system that is supposed to educate children in the topics of reading, writing, math, etc. A large portion of you reading this book most likely send your children to public school for education. You trust they will learn the basic education they need so they can be successful in life and will graduate with the ability to pursue whatever career they choose. You expect they will be adequately equipped to continue whatever education might be required for any possible line of work they desire.

For the most part, public education does accomplish this goal. The problem comes when parents turn their complete trust over to the public system and do not completely understand the scope of topics their school board and government have now decided they are responsible to teach our children.

If you are anything like me, you have probably found you are not in complete agreement with the government about every topic; in fact, in America, Christian values are no longer embraced by our government. As for my husband and I, we were extremely blessed to have a church school to send our children to, and I am a strong supporter of Christian education. I do, however, understand this option is not practical, or reliable, for everyone. I even understand there are some parents who feel strongly about sending their children to public school to be a light in the darkness. So, at this point, I want to clearly state that I am NOT against public education, but I do believe that regardless of where your child goes to school, the ultimate responsibility for what they are being taught falls on you. God did not give the mandate to your government to train your child, He gave that mandate to you. Please, do not blindly trust their education to anyone else. You are responsible to know what your child is being taught.

We have a saying at our church regarding education that illuminates this idea: "If you turn your children over to Caesar to educate, don't be surprised when they return as Romans." Throughout history, governments have taken it upon themselves to set many different agendas for training youth. A big agenda our own government has taken on right now is sexuality and the freedom to choose who or, perhaps eventually, what you can love. It even believes that children should have the right to choose their own gender and identify as whichever sex they choose. Now, if you as a parent are not staying on top of this type of educational agenda, and the fact that the government is beginning to teach this sex education to kindergarteners, than you may find yourself very surprised when your little boy comes home one day to tell you he is really a girl stuck in a boy's body.

Adolf Hitler has been quoted as saying, "He alone who owns the youth gains the future." He was also noted to have said, "If I tell you a big enough lie and tell it frequently enough, it will be believed." Hitler may have said these things, but they are not original to him; he basically rephrased "train up a child in the way he should go and when he is old, he will not depart from it." Also, it sounds like he knew 1 Peter 5:8: "Be alert and of sober mind, your enemy, the devil prowls around like a roaring lion looking for someone to devour." The Scripture informs us he is able to do this by convincing us to believe his lies. God is the one who first told His people the importance of training their children. He also stressed that we make sure they know truth, talking about it while sitting at home and as we are walking along. He even said to write it on the door post. God also warned us about the power of the enemy's lies.

Most Christians can be very trusting people, and sometimes we trust so much that we simply cannot believe our own government could have an agenda for our children and insert it into their education behind our backs. The problem is I am pretty sure there were a lot of stunned German parents when they heard their own children spouting hatred directed toward their Jewish neighbors.

Governments, like ours, that claim to be based in Christian-based nations do have agendas. Sadly, some of those agendas come from very ungodly people who can spout a big lie long enough to convince people it is truth. Governments are run by people, and people have their own agendas, some of which are in direct opposition to the Word of God. So know what your children are being taught. Be sure to counter the lies with the truth of God. Tell your children what God says and be sure you surround them with the truth. I know you cannot sit through every class your child takes, but do your research. Know the latest education mandate, know what your children's textbooks say, and most importantly, talk to your children about what they are learning. Don't be afraid to ask the hard questions.

I have mostly talked about public education, but Jerry and I took this command from God into every opportunity that included sources of outside influence on our children. When my boys played sports and had coaches I did not know, I never just dropped them off at practice or a game and picked them up later. No, if I didn't know that person, I brought my folding chair and wrapped up in blankets and sat there through every practice. If other children needed rides, I gave them. My child was going to be protected and covered in every situation. Don't get me wrong, I had a million things I could have been doing. I was a very busy working mom with three kids, but those three kids were my first and foremost responsibility.

Another place where our children come under attack is through TV and movies. I don't remember the source of this information, possibly a child development study, but when I learned this tidbit, it totally changed the way I watched shows with my children. The information I am referring to is that children do not have the ability an adult has to sort through information as it comes in and then pick and choose fact from fiction. So you see, as you watch a movie and something is said that is not true, your adult brain throws that information out; your child's brain does not. Even worse, if you are watching something untrue with your child and say nothing, they assume it is okay. Children's minds are sponges, so they take each statement as a whole and accept it all. My silence tells my child I approve of the information being presented. I was shocked after I began to watch TV and movies with this new lens. From that point on, we began the habit of stopping a movie mid-sentence if needed to make sure our children understood the statement they'd just heard was not true. We were not always the popular people to sit around in a movie theater because we pointed out the lies. We were also not afraid to get up and walk out of a movie. We could handle our child's disappointment because preventing their disappointment was not as important as preventing their heads from being filled with trash.

Most parents grew up on Disney and totally trusted the company, but if you pay attention, Disney can be a parent's worst enemy. You will notice a common theme in most Disney productions. They promote the notion that parents cannot be trusted, because they do not understand their children. Parents are selfish and only want their own way causing the child to rebel. After rebelling to show the parent who is righ the parent come around to apologize for not paying enough attention to the child. Kids are always right and the parents are stupid and frequently need their children to save them. My husband calls it the "Doofus Dad" syndrome. These productions portray leaders as clueless, selfish idiots, or even worse, as the bad guys. Pay attention, parents, because rebellion is glorified and even rewarded.

I remember when Amy was a baby, Disney's *The Little Mermaid* came out, and I rented it. I was so impressed, at first, because it seemed to be telling the Christ story: dad tells his child to stay away from something, she rebels because she thinks she knows better, and she even makes a deal with the witch (devil) to get what she wants. She later realizes the deal she made has her trapped in the witches clutches, so then her dad gives his own life to earn her freedom. It was the story of our rebellion and sin costing the Father everything, such that He pays with Himself for our redemption. It seemed like a great movie until they ruined it when daddy went to his daughter and repented for not listening to her. What? Her rebellion cost his life and he repents? Yes, he repented because if he had only listened to her and understood her heart, she wouldn't have needed to rebel. I was so mad that the video almost didn't make it back to the rental place. I had to restrain myself from destroying it. This theme is very common in Disney productions.

The last point I want to make in this chapter is to say be sure you always listen to the Holy Spirit for your children. They are first and foremost God's children, so if you listen, He will help you. If either Jerry or I had a check in our spirit about anything related to our children, we stopped, listened, and obeyed. It did not matter what it was. If we felt like we should not let our child go to a birthday party, a sleepover, or not to use a certain babysitter, we listened and obeyed. One of our dear friends told us a story we never forgot. He said when he drove his son to college to drop him off in another town, he felt like he heard God say to not leave him there because if he did he would lose him. He talked himself out of it and brushed it off. After all, his son was going to college and his faith should have been set by now. He later regretted not obeying at that moment because while at college his son turned away from God and embraced homosexuality. At the time I write this book, our friend has gone on to be with Jesus, but his son still professes to be an atheist. That father's pain was so deep, and I do not ever want to experience anything like it.

My biggest story about the Holy Spirit's care for our children began when my little girl was about four years old. I had just started letting her go outside by herself to play in the yard with the neighbor kids. I was doing some house cleaning when I heard, or more accurately felt the Holy Spirit say, "Go outside. Someone is going to take Amy." Thank God I responded. I walked to the front door where I could see

Amy and the neighbor girl sitting on the porch swing. The neighbor's boys were on their bikes in the yard. All of a sudden, the neighbor boy said, "Someone's here." As I stepped out onto the porch, two men were headed into the yard. When they saw me, they jumped back into their car and sped away. Thank you Jesus! If I had ignored the Holy Spirit, I don't know if I could have lived with what might have happened. I may never know why God said "No" to some things for our children; all I needed to know is that He did say "No" and, praise God. we obeyed.

JERRY

Knowing what your children are being taught involves monitoring on two levels: watching both the stuff that's coming in and how the stuff is affecting them. In both cases, prayer, the Holy Spirit's guidance, and teamwork are necessities. Debbie and I are blessed with complimentary interests and skills which aided us in these two challenges. We had frequent conversations about our priorities and how to shuffle activities, wants, and needs so we were adequately monitoring the flow. Finding the time to investigate the stuff coming in was difficult for me, and fortunately, Debbie taught at the school the kids attended and had access to the textbooks and teachers, which afford her snapshots of what was happening on a regular basis. My schedule did not allow me to be as involved in the children's day-to-day activities, but whenever possible I would leave work early or use my time off to take the kids to their events and sit, watch, listen, evaluate, and process what was happening so I could talk with them later. I echo what Debbie mentioned about TV and movies and extended it into reading some of the books they were reading so I knew what was silently being fed into their brains.

Engaging them to share their responses and insight as to what was being pumped into their brains took lots of time and patience. At first, I always wanted to get straight to the point, get the details, realign them, then move on. Most six-year-olds don't respond well to that technique. They want you to value them, not treat them as a project. Taking the time to understand how your child thinks and what is their perspective of the world is vital. One child might be very intent on making sure everyone in the class likes them, another child might be more interested in always getting every answer correct on a test, and another might be hesitant to share in fear of getting himself or someone else in trouble. When discussing their day, understanding what is important to them makes it easier to build trust and gain insight into how their environment is affecting them. Like most humans, children will not engage in a vulnerable conversation if they do not feel respected, trust that their ideas will be respected, know that what they value will not be maligned, and that they will not be attacked if they do something wrong or believe something differently than you. This is not to say that you should passively ignore troublesome ideas or actions, but you do need to respect your children's dignity when addressing it. There were times I had to firmly tell my children that they were in error, then draw a map on how they were to correct the error. Whenever possible, I tried to discover if they recognized the error before I identified it. Gentle questioning to feel out what they encountered that day was part of our nightly debriefing; some nights more extensive than others.

Do not try to trick them into giving you information. If they haven't noticed it on the first couple attempts, your children will shortly, then they will resent being manipulated. I told them I was asking questions because I cared about them and it was my job to help them process their world. It was challenging at times to not explode and fix the problem immediately, but those times I was able to patiently walk with them through the stuff of their day and watch the lights turn on to see them come to their own godly conclusions were very rewarding. By patient, I don't mean fifteen minutes; I mean sometimes a few days of fifteen to twenty minute conversations daily, working through the emotions and misconceptions, was necessary to get there.

For most kids, getting in trouble is high on their list of things to avoid with not wanting to fail ranking close by. If your inquiries trap them, or your answers shame them, or their honesty frequently results in punishment, you will have difficulty maintaining open communication. I tried very hard to make sure my children understood the difference between being punished for a rebellious action versus being corrected for an action that resulted in a bad outcome versus just wanting to understand what they were thinking. I tried to promote correction as a positive: we are addressing this problem and changing something about it so you can succeed. I tried to build a connection so they wanted to tell me about what they were learning and doing. When they hesitated to tell me what they were thinking or did not want to share what had happened, it usually involved their fear of being punished or being told they failed. I tried to always steer our discussions and conclusions away from these two outcomes. Frequently, they were afraid that if they repeated what the teacher had said, they would be in trouble for betraying her or, if they revealed something that they were doing, I would not want them to continue and then their friends would make fun of them.

Allowing time for them to ramble about what they find interesting without challenging them and asking genuine questions that encourage them to expound even more may result in hours of conversations about video games, Legos, book characters, etc., but it shows that you are interested in them, not purely bent on fixing them. I recommend praying for wisdom to discern how to respond when their opinions are different from yours. Allowing them to express their opinions, and validating their autonomy, also builds connection for further conversations. Be aware there are times when their opinions are contrary to God and dangerous. Be gentle and respectful in how you attempt to turn that ship, taking special care to make sure the differences are worth addressing. Looking back, chastising Michael because he liked the St. Louis Rams instead of the Kansas City Chiefs was not my best day. We eventually "matured" into teasing each other about our woeful teams rather than being hurt because the other did not respect our choice.

Even though it seems like an impossible task, you can safely monitor what is coming into your child's life and either stop the bad stuff or help them to process it. Trying to get kids to be open and honest about their lives has to be one of the most common difficulties parents face. Adopting a mindset that respects your child as a valuable, interesting child of God and not as a problem you are forced to deal with is the beginning place for a secure relationship that fosters conversation. You will still have to correct and punish, but even in that, honoring them as a treasured part of your life communicates that you view them as important and meaningful individuals.

CHAPTER 8
WHAT TO DO WHEN YOU MESS UP

DEBBIE

One of my fears when God began to speak to us about writing this book was that you might get the impression we either did everything perfectly or we somehow thought we did. Nothing could be farther from the truth. In fact, we both had our own moments of arguing with God and saying, "Why us?" The problem was, as it usually is with God, He did not really want our opinion on this; He just wanted us to obey. So, at this point, I would like to say there is only one perfect parent and that is our Father, God. Jerry and I would be the very first people to tell you we've made our share of mistakes, but thankfully we have a God who can even use our mistakes because He is bigger than them. In fact, some of the Burbee family jokes are centered around some of our blunders. It is healthy to laugh at yourself sometimes, and believe me, we do that a lot in our house.

When we decided to have children, we both knew we would make some mistakes. But the cry of our hearts was to have a legacy on this earth that would be found serving Jesus on the day of His return. We also, as I mentioned, knew God was bigger than any mistake we could make. God had placed in our hearts a parenting blueprint from His word, and we believed He would be faithful to His promises if we remained faithful. We also knew that the Bible tells us God does not leave us alone, He has given us His Spirit to guide us. We believed He would guide us through all of our mistakes as well as show us His desire for our children. On our part, we would need to remain humble, submitted, and prayerful.

Over and over, Jerry and I have tried to encourage you by telling you that you have got this. We are not changing that statement at all in this chapter, but we would be deficient if we did not also tell you that there will be times when you will mess up. The key to handling these times is also a Bible principle. The same way we make things right before God when we mess up, through repentance, is the way we should handle things when we mess up with our children. It is a mistake to think that repentance shows your children weakness. It is just the opposite. It takes a strong person to admit wrong and ask for forgiveness. When our children see us come to them, humbly admit our failure, and ask them to forgive us, it actually increases their respect for us.

Sometimes as parents I think we fool ourselves into thinking our children will not notice if we are living contrary to what we are teaching them. Truthfully, though, our children pay a lot more attention to what we do than to what we say, and our words are only impactive as they watch us do what we have taught them to do. One of the best ways to frustrate your children is to live contrary to what you are telling them to do. This is then compounded if we begin to punish them for something they see us do. The classic example for my generation was having parents who punished us for smoking when they were two-pack-a-day smokers themselves.

There are several reasons why you may blow it with your children. For me, some of my worst moments came when I got overwhelmed by all the responsibilities of life, like being the best wife, mother, teacher, housekeeper, church leader, etc. I remember how on Saturday when I began trying to catch up with my housework, my children would start playing in the room I had just finished cleaning and of course would be making it a mess again. My frustration would boil over at my sweet children. I give this as an example of a situation in which I could have justified my actions. I knew yelling at them was wrong, and when I did, something inside of me would cringe, but it happened every time. When I had recognition of my sin, I would then collect myself and go to them and to ask forgiveness. Sometimes though, in the moment of our sin, we do not always see it. But I discovered if I would stay humble before God, He would come and shine light on my actions so I could go make things right. I'm no different than any of you; sometimes I wanted to make excuses to God and complain about all I had to do, but none of that could justify my sin, and deep inside I knew that. At those times, I would hear Jesus speak to me gently just like the time He did with Martha when she felt overwhelmed and He reminded her that Mary had chosen the more perfect thing. Jesus would remind me that somewhere my priorities had gotten off track.

Sometimes for women the root of most of our frustrations in life come from getting our priorities wrong. When I forget who I am, a daughter of the Most High God, I lose sight of what is important. God says that as His daughter I am perfect just as I am. Whenever I have lost sight of this, I attempted to prove my worth to others, and maybe to myself, by trying to DO all these things to be accepted. When I was spending time in His presence, it was easier to keep the truth of what God says in my spirit and not become so pressured to DO or BE anything but His.

We women seem to have this image in our mind of what the perfect woman of God looks like, you know that Proverbs 31 woman where the Kings mother is describing the perfect wife deserving of honor. She seems to be able to do anything and everything with perfection. We read those scriptures and somehow are sure we do not measure up, but that is not true and not what God says about you or me. He says we are perfectly made. He says we are made with purpose, and we can only keep that purpose clear when we spend time with Him. Jesus is our reason for living. At the age of sixty-one, I can tell you that over the many years of my life when I was faithful to spending time in the presence of God my life went so much smoother. Now, I'm not saying there were no problems. Wrong, the Bible doesn't promise that. What I am saying is that through every moment I knew that whether the path was smooth or rocky my God was both with me and proud of me. Losing sight of that can cause women to quickly become overwhelmed, and that is a setup for failing your children in your busyness and frustration.

Even when you keep your priorities straight, you will have times when you miss it. When that happens, you need to take the lead and run to your child to ask for forgiveness. I will tell you sometimes when we were having one of these mommy repentance moments my children would be so touched they would open up and we would have some of the best conversations about every type of topic. I think that when my children saw me humble myself and show my own weakness, as well as my desire to follow Jesus, they felt like they could do the same with me and open up about their own struggles of just being human.

That brings me to the second part of the process. True repentance should produce fruit, so be sure to not only repent but make sure to make the necessary changes to make things right. Repentance in and of itself means to completely turn from the direction you are moving and head the right way. If your actions do not change, then you have not repented, you have just said sorry. Now sorry is nice, but if nothing changes, then it does not take long for sorry to lose all meaning. Now, returning to my example of cleaning on Saturday and yelling at my children, I still had to clean but the change made was that when I started cleaning, my children would play upstairs in their rooms and we were both happier. (But believe me I would have rather been playing with them instead of cleaning.)

As your children get older, you may find that occasionally God might use one of them to bring conviction. Our youngest son, Joe, has done this more than once for me. He is a very black and white thinker. Right is right and wrong is wrong. and if he saw us do something that was inconsistent with the way we had always done things, he would come to us and ask why. Our son was never doing this to cause us trouble; he was really curious as to why we were doing something different. Most of the time that would open my eyes to my own inconsistencies and the need to repent to Joe and correct our actions.

Being honest with your children to repent to them and make things right calls for a lot of transparency with them. Due to that fact, I feel like I need to give a caution to moms. Moms, your children are NEVER your confidants. You may spend all your time with them and, as they get older, feel like they are friends but you are still the parent and they are your children. That means you have to have other women in your life that you can confide in. Never pull your children into adult issues. Their brains are not mature enough to handle that. And when you are at odds with your husband, the rule is you never talk to your child about their dad, but always keep talking with your spouse about them.

My summation is know who you are, be confident in God's love for you, spend time with Him, be humble, listen for correction, and be quick to repent, and let your repentance produce noticeable fruit in your life. Only God is perfect, but He has made a path for us to be like Him. God's mercies are new every morning, and His faithfulness to us when we obey His commands will never fail.

JERRY

If I were to see the title of this chapter in another book, my first thought would be, "I need to hear this because I mess up all the time." Then pondering on it a bit longer my next thought would be, "What do they mean by 'mess up?'"

In regards to the first thought, mistakes will happen. Who out there has had their infant roll off the changing table? Or, hadn't realized their youngster had learned to crawl and left him on the living room floor and thirty seconds later he is tumbling down the stairs? Or, shut your six-year-old in the sliding door of the minivan? Those are in my "Dad's Greatest Blunders" album, and thus far, I have not noticed any long-term effects.

Moving to the second thought, we use "mess up" to refer to both mistakes and sin. Dumping my infant out of her car seat so she could execute a very poor forward roll was a mistake. Chastising my eight-year-old son because I did not think his prayer was fervent enough was a sin. Blunders, oopses, "I forgot," and "that did not go as planned" are all mistakes and require acknowledgment of the pain they may have inflicted and usually some type of resolution, but I put them in a lesser category than breaking my vow to love my children. Messing up means you have done something harmful or negligent, but making a mistake is not the same as sin. Each requires a response, but discerning the difference is important. If we love as Jesus loved, sin is less likely, yet forgetting a promise or accidentally mowing over a prized toy are not sin, that is depending upon how we react.

Aiming to love as Jesus loved is hopefully the goal we all have in mind, so let's look again at the fruit of the Spirit from Galatians 5 and the 1 Corinthians 13 description of love. These are not rules as much as they are compass settings. If you stop and think you may have wandered off course, consult this compass to regain your bearings. If you want to know which direction to head, use both these scriptures.

Galatians 5

- *love*
- *joy*
- *peace*
- *forbearance*
- *kindness*
- *goodness*
- *faithfulness*
- *gentleness*
- *self-control*

1 Corinthians 13:4-8

- *Love is patient.*
- *Love is kind.*

- *It does not envy.*
- *It does not boast.*
- *It is not proud.*
- *It does not dishonor others.*
- *It is not self-seeking.*
- *It is not easily angered.*
- *It keeps no record of wrongs.*
- *Love does not delight in evil but rejoices with the truth.*
- *It always protects.*
- *It always trusts.*
- *It always hopes.*
- *It always perseveres.*
- *Love never fails.*

Books have been written about these scriptures, and I would not do justice to each item listed if I tried to summarize them here. These are the reference points and possibilities provided by the Bible. If needed, meditate on each one for a day or so, asking God to awaken these qualities within you. Don't move too quickly from this spot. These words are very familiar to anyone who has been in the church for any period of time, but we need to pause and soak them in like it's the first time we have we discovered them. Think about your children. What's your posture toward them? Do they take forever to do the simplest things? Are they frustrating or a joy? Again, these passages are not intended to heap condemnation on a weary parent, they are what is possible while living in the Spirit. Messing up that turns into sin usually occurs when we haven't used this compass as our guide.

Yelling at your child when frustrated with their behavior, scolding them harshly in front of their friends, and similar actions are examples of wandering off the path and they resemble the deeds of the flesh, fits of rage, and malice. The deeds of the flesh from Galatians 5: 19-21 are listed as:

- *Sexual immorality*
- *Impurity and debauchery*
- *Idolatry and witchcraft*

75

- *Hatred*
- *Discord*
- *Jealousy*
- *Fits of rage*
- *Selfish ambition*
- *Dissension*
- *Factions and envy*
- *Drunkenness, orgies, and the like*

These are the actions and emotions that are sin and repentance is necessary; not "I'm sorry" but a change in behavior and restitution if appropriate. Again, don't move too quickly. Ask the Holy Spirit to open your eyes and your heart.

What Debbie said about repentance is vital. Finding out that I needed to repent does not always come from a moment of radiance with an angelic "AAHHHHH" being harmonized in the background. A lot of times it was revealed to me by others, such as my wife, friends, or kids. When receiving correction, I try to humbly allow the person to communicate their concern. I do not have to agree with them, but I do not need to feel condemned. I strive to hear the voice of the Spirit in the message delivered. What specific thing is being addressed? What influence is pride and defensiveness having upon their presentation and my reception? Do I see the sin? What is the appropriate repentance? I also try to have a conversation about the event so I can better understand what happened and how the people involved were affected. Finding the balance of being quick to repent but not easily condemned is challenging but possible.

Because I know I make mistakes, I have tried to maintain an atmosphere that is open to suggestions, even from my children; specifically in how I receive correction from my children. More than likely, if they are the ones who were hurt, in some manner they will be the ones who demonstrate the effects of my action. Younger children usually are not mature enough to verbalize what they are feeling but their feelings can be noticed in their responses to you. They might not be as warm, they might act out more, or they may have harsh responses when told to do something. Older kids may have the ability to describe what happened but they may not have the maturity to package it well, and we might make the error of responding to their poor delivery rather than to the substance of what they are saying. This nearsightedness increases the conflict and erodes the trust on both sides. I have wanted to use my life as a guide for my children on how to respond to criticism, exhortation, and frustration. I want to have a relationship where we can peacefully discuss the issue and work through it. At different age levels, this looks different, takes some trial and error, often requires specific input from seasoned parents, and prayer.

Over the years, I noticed a difference in my kids' posture and demeanor that helped me determine "Did I make a mistake? "or "Did I sin?" When they were disappointed or hurt by my blunder, they were merely upset; their disappointment or sadness was draped over a rigid frame that begrudgingly accepted what had transpired. When I sinned against them, they were deflated inside and their sadness was draped over a mud puddle. This observation was not all that I used to determine my answer to the questions above, but insight such as this one helped me to ask questions to gain better discernment over what was happening. This phenomenon was not one born in my brilliance; it came as a gift from the Spirit. He will provide something similar for you if you ask, listen, and obey. Once I realized what had happened, I would check myself: a simple prayer asking for God's help to hear His voice, then asking for insight into what was going on with my child. Sometimes this went better than it did at other times. I wanted to model to my children how to humbly receive criticism while also training them how to communicate that they had been violated as well as showing different approaches of how to do that. I did not tolerate disrespect or rebellion, but I did have to acknowledge that they felt I had disrespected them, so we needed to carefully discuss those differences. I tried to avoid the confrontation being "I'm right; you're wrong." Instead, I attempted to step back from the emotions, though without ignoring them, and analyze what happened through the lens of the Scripture.

It may sound like I am describing a polished, refined process, but it was never this neat or organized. Lots of bumps had to be navigated to stay on track. The ditches on either side of this approach are: 1) The child does not feel the security, freedom, respect, or trust to approach you about your mistakes, and 2) The child feels permission to rebel and disrespect you because they perceive they have been disrespected. Neither are good. Some of the pain our children feel when we mess up can manifest as quietness, anger, avoidance, depression, snarkiness, and grumbling, making it our job to sift through their immaturity to find the true source of their behavior.

Realizing that messing up was inevitable, I used to console myself with "You are going to screw up; just try not to screw up really bad." This is not bad advice, but its "oh, well" attitude seems to make bad behavior acceptable and that no repentance or recovery is necessary. Looking back, I think better self-advice would have been a simpler "be real." I plan to live Christ-like, but I accept what happens as an opportunity for Him to purify my heart and glorify Him in my response to the situation. It is His move to bring purity. As the kids got older and I saw the shallowness of my original advice, I reached deep in an effort to live "being real". Warning: being real is not permission to do what you want and expect everyone else to absorb the consequences; being real means you see yourself as God sees you and you see others as He sees them. That is real. Correction and encouragement from the Spirit kept me between the ditches when I would listen. My mindset fully accepted I would make mistakes. My pride was not always helpful in allowing the appropriate response to those mistakes. My fear attempted to minimize the impact of my sins. My self-deception tried to convince me that my impatience was good for my kids because it built their character and toughened them up. Now, I would advise my younger self, "Enjoy your wife, enjoy your life, enjoy your kids, and enjoy the Spirit's leading. Be real."

Parenting is messy. Still some well-placed, beautiful brush strokes reveal the image of God, even when our grimy fingerprints have smudged some of the finer details. Our children are works of art, and as apprentices to the Master Artist, we parents will misshape aspects of the image we are trying to portray. However, the Master is constantly watching our work and steps in to correct our errors or walks us through how to correct them ourselves. Don't freak out when something goes wrong but don't ignore errors either. When you mess up, look for God's way to fix it.

CHAPTER 9
REBELLION

DEBBIE

The one tool the devil has that he can use against us anytime he wants is his words. The Bible tells us that the devil is a liar, yet far too often we believe every word he says. Sometimes we even go so far as to make one of his lies into a well-accepted norm in our culture. One of those lies which I believe we have made an acceptable norm in America is that teenage rebellion is normal. Think about it: can you support that statement with any Biblical facts? Now, I've read my Bible through several times and I can say I've never seen one scripture that supports the idea that teenagers rebelling is normal. In fact, all rebellion is condemned.

In the Church, our children can grow up to love and honor their parents and not have to rebel into sin. I really hope you believe me when I tell you this. My children never said the words "I hate you" or "You are ruining my life." In fact, my daughter came home from a friend's house overwhelmed because she was stunned at how her friend talked to, and about, her parents.

Since the devil's theory about rebellion in children is a lie, I have my own theory about a child that has begun to change their behavior in a manner that is outside of their previously demonstrated character. If this happens with your child it is a cry for help because something is very wrong in their life and they don't know how to tell you they need help. I'm not talking about that individual rebellious act that needs discipline in a moment I'm talking about a complete behavior change that continues over a period of time.

When my children were little, I noticed every time they were close to making a breakthrough concerning something in their lives, they would get really frustrated and be very fussy. If you have children already, think back to when they were babies. Right before they learned to crawl, did they become fussy? Mine did. Right before learning to walk, right before learning to talk and say words, they became frustrated and generally fussy. Then a breakthrough would come and they were happy again. Well, I believe that as children get older that fussy stage starts looking like rebellion.

Now, I have never seen any scientific studies on this, probably because Satan has convinced us it is normal, but I have an example from my own life. I grew up in Church. I remember having conversations with God as young as four. I was baptized at eight years old. In my child's mind, this was the time I publicly let everyone know I was going to live my life for God. I was also the good child in my home. My older sister (four years older) would get into trouble a lot. I was that kid who would listen to her fight with my parents and say to myself, "Ok, so if I don't do that, I won't get in trouble." In fact, I had very few memories of getting in trouble. But for most of my childhood, I had someone in my life who was very abusive to me. The abuse was both physical and emotional. My abuser told me almost daily that I was fat and ugly and enlisted the neighborhood kids to help make fun of me. The abuse was physical too but not sexual, thank God. I will spare you the specifics, but as a child I felt trapped in a horrible situation and could not see any relief in sight.

It seemed like the abuse was at its highest when I was in junior high school, which for us was 7th and 8th grade. That was the one time in my life that this good, little girl became rebellious. For one thing, I became anorexic. Then I started lying all the time. I was going out with friends and we would meet up with boys even though I wasn't supposed to date until I was sixteen.,. I would yell at my mom and tell her I hated her. My doctor placed me on Xanax, a strong anti-anxiety medicine, and he told my mom I was depressed. In truth, I needed my parents' help so badly. I wanted them to push in; to find out why their perfect little girl had become a monster. Unfortunately help did not come for me because my mother believed Satan's lie that I was going through a " normal stage". She thought that if we lived through these days I would eventually outgrow my behavior.

Satan's "fact" that rebellion is normal teenager behavior makes most parents back off, hoping to just survive until their child outgrows it as my mom did. My theory, and I believe it is supported by God, is that if your child is acting out, that is the time to push in, not back off. Pursue that child. Do whatever it takes to make sure she knows you are there for her, no matter what. Do not give up. Pray like never before and do all you can to get your child to talk. Remove your child from bad influences in their lives. Rebellion pulls your child out from under your covering. The enemy does not have to go through you to get to your child. You can bet he has placed some bad influences in their life. This is often when children are exposed to drugs, alcohol, sex, and homosexuality. I was exposed to some of these things, but for me the strong heart I had for God protected me by His grace. I will say, in my story, the one area my mom fought for me was the anorexia. I believe she literally prayed me out of it. I look back and wish she had pressed in to find out why, but God was faithful.

When I entered high school, I had completely dropped all my bad friends and was back to Church. I was also back to being my parent's good girl. You see, my abuser had moved away and no longer had access to me. I was free in more ways than one, but the point of my story is my rebellion was a cry for help.

I have also watched this pattern in other children and have found my theory runs true. God placed our children under our protection and covering. That covering doesn't end when they become teenagers. If you are wondering if there ever comes a time with your children when you can sit back and coast, my answer is not until they are adults and they leave your house. Even then, if you are like me, they will still occupy a huge amount of your prayer time.

I have talked about rebellion with teenagers, but it can happen at any age. Children do not always know how to tell you something is wrong. They also may not even realize they are crying out for help, but deep inside they are. Do whatever it takes to keep the enemy of their souls from getting them. This is where dying for your child is put to the test. Almost every parent I have talked with says they would die for their child. Well, you may not have a gun pointed at your head; the dying here is to die to selfish desires. How much is your child's life worth?

My prayer is that you never, never have to experience this. Unfortunately, we live in a world that has even brought pornography to the phone or computer your child carries. As parents, we must be more diligent than ever. Take every thought captive to Jesus and even if the world says something is normal, look to the ultimate source of truth, the Word of God, as your standard. The devil prowls around like a roaring lion. Let's do everything we can to expose him for the liar he is and protect our children.

They are worth it!

JERRY

Debbie did a great job of identifying a pattern we have seen that too often goes unrecognized. We were constantly praying for discernment; please do the same. The ability to determine when your child needs help, a rebuke, or encouragement is at the foundation of parenting. This important distinction will guide how you approach your rebellious child, but more importantly, it influences the outcome of future relationships both relationship with you and with others in their life. Determining between thoughtless acts versus defiant rejection versus a cry for help, and responding appropriately, can carry the weight of your child's future.

When I was little, we lived in an old house that had a towel bar made of porcelain. It was very elegant, Victorian-looking, and matched the rest of the house, but it was not very sturdy, especially when a five-year-old is trying to do pull ups. My dad warned me several times not to hang from it.

"Son, you are too heavy, and if you hang from the bar, you are going to break it."

"Yes, Dad."

I was verbally agreeable and well-intentioned, but my rambunctious nature and short memory proved fatal for the towel bar. One evening, as I was washing up for supper, I impulsively grabbed the bar and let my full weight bear down on it. As predicted by my father, the bar snapped. As I scrambled up from the floor, each hand holding a portion of the bar, my dad's words flooded back into my consciousness. I was devastated. Or more correctly, I was scared. My dad had little patience with disobedience, and I had seen his wrath meet my brothers' defiance many times. I was in trouble. My mind raced to find an explanation that would be acceptable, but the lack of creativity and the fear of being caught in a lie squelched any reasonable story. I went downstairs to the kitchen where my dad was, bawling like my dog had been run over by a train, and confessed to the incident. I don't remember his words (my memory is poor when I am in extreme panic) but I think he brushed it aside and said we would deal with it after supper. Again, I don't remember that meal (the panic and memory thing again) but afterwards he took me to his work area in the basement. "You broke it. You can help me fix it."

My dad found a dowel rod. We took it up to the bathroom and made sure it was the right diameter, then measured the length we needed to cut. Back down to the basement we went where we cut it. He then grabbed a can of white paint and a brush, we went back up the stairs, and he fit the dowel into the bar holder. After opening the paint can, he handed me the brush and stepped back. My fear meter was in the red zone and I wasn't sure what was happening. Where was the yelling? The harsh words about being irresponsible? I did not receive even a stern look.

Over the years, this story has surfaced in my memory when thinking about my relationship with my dad, my relationship with God, and my relationship with my children. All three relationships are tied together and each of them influences the perspective I have towards the others. My dad displayed great discernment and self-control while demonstrating the grace and mercy of our Father. It is a reference point I return to frequently. My fear was so great that I did not expect such a tender, yet corrective response. Since then, I have realized I once had the same attitude about my relationship with God—"I disobeyed and He is going to thrash me"—only to be met with tender correction wrapped in grace and mercy. At one particular dark point in finding my way with God, I blamed my dad for allowing me to get away with sin. He should have thrashed me, that way I wouldn't be so nonchalant about trifling with God's law. I wished he would have ingrained the fear of the Father so deep in me that I would never disobey again. Then I had my own children and was horrified to think that my children would be as scared of my love as I was of my dad's love. Even worse was that I had felt that way towards God and that I could lead my children into a similar relationship with Him.

As Debbie pointed out, rebellion is always sin. Disobedience is a violation and does carry consequences. God does not tolerate those who refuse to adhere to His requirements. Our children must know this fact: He is boss and what He says is how things will be. If we ignore Him and live by our own rules, we will meet His wrath. But we also must know, and demonstrate to our kids, that He is patient, merciful, and gracious in His correction, and that His correction is restorative. We can emulate that.

When rebellion occurs, we need the discernment of God to guide our response. Some rebellion is like my impulsive towel bar incident. It needs to be addressed so that the child knows he is loved but also that there are consequences to the wanton action. When rebellion is being used as a tool to express distress or get attention, like Debbie referred to, it can be very effective at disrupting the entire family. If not confronted wisely, it can be similar to Moses striking the rock: from

86

our own frustration, we misrepresent the Father's heart and display a disobedience of our own.

While society has erroneously tried to call rebellion normal, we must recognize our children will sin. They will rebel. They will struggle. Our response must be clear and definitive at representing God's heart. We need His discernment. Firm correction can still be loving. Mercy may require restitution. Rebellion and sin cannot be ignored, but not every fire is controlled by blasting it with water. We can use their sin as an opportunity to teach, as an object lesson of how the Father's love is displayed.

It seems there is also confusion between growing pains and rebellion. Not every disagreement is rebellion. Not every variation from the family norm is defiance. As children explore who they are and what is important to them, they need the freedom to venture into areas you have not roamed. As mentioned before, I wrestled hard with this question when Michael declared at age eight that he was a Rams fan.

"Wait. This family has been Chiefs' fans for generations; your father and his father before him. We have always been loyal to Arrowhead, despite years of mediocrity. The only reason you would defy me is that you must be rebellious."

It sounds ludicrous now, but at the time I really wrestled with his motivation. I was not going to allow any weeds of rebellion to have any chance to grow in his heart. But God granted me the discernment that this was Michael's way of expressing his individuality. He was not defiant; he was opinionated.

I felt it was very necessary to identify when my children were straying. I tried hard to identify the action that to me looked rebellious, without drawing a conclusion too quickly, but still be quick to stomp on anything that had the smell of rebellion. While Michael's opinion about football teams was not rebellion, there were many other declarations that were and were confronted as such. Amy can be very definitive when she has formed an opinion. As a youngster, she was not shy about letting Debbie know when she disagreed with one of her decisions. When Amy was in college, she lived at home but was as busy as a college student could be and I didn't see her as frequently as before. I had not considered that she would develop any opinions about God that did not originate from me, and when she began to express these opinions, it was quite concerning. I concluded she had become a liberal millennial who was being seduced to the dark side. Fortunately, God worked out a time where she and I could regularly meet and talk. After enduring a couple of my rants about her not resisting the temptations of the wicked ways of the world, she bravely sought to communicate her heart. She assured me she had not given up the core elements of Christianity, but she did have a different perspective toward some of them than I had. After several months of vigorous conversations, she actually revealed some things about God I had not seen or considered. Instead of being a rebellious, liberal millennial, she had become a woman of God.

Rebellion is a sign something is wrong in your child's life. It is a symptom that points to a deeper issue; either they don't understand something about you and God, they are careless, or they are distressed. However, it cannot be permitted to remain. It has to be rooted out and dealt with. Our best parenting occurred when we worked with our children to determine the dysfunction and together sought God for a solution. Rebellion can easily create an us versus them atmosphere, which is the enemy sowing discord and trying to destroy. If we were nurturing a relationship of respect with the particular child, it was much easier for us all to identify the rebellion and the deeper cause, which led to the relationship between all of us and God flourishing. Sometimes firm boundaries have to be enforced and mercy is displayed by not allowing sin to run rampant. Sometimes the strain is not rebellion, but a child trying to find their wings. Appeals to God for the wisdom to know the difference and the knowledge of how to respond to each situation was the daily bread of our parenting. Crushing their individuality in the name of thwarting rebellion can be devastating, and that is certainly not the goal.

Please pray for discernment. Normal is a hard thing to define, but avoid the folly that a rebellious child has to be tolerated. As the Father has loved you, so love your children.

CHAPTER 10
SIBLING RIVALRY

DEBBIE

Another topic dear to my heart when it comes to children is sibling rivalry. I had been told by a lot of people that siblings fighting or having issues with each other was harmless, even normal and to be expected. Yet I have seen over the years, siblings do great harm to each other all under the masquerade of sibling rivalry. The devil can use a sibling's words to do incredible damage to a child's feelings of having value. My sister was older than I was, and as the kid-sister, I really looked up to her and longed for her to tell me that she liked me or thought I was a valuable person. I don't think I was any different from other children in this respect. Every child inherently knows in their heart that family is supposed to love you. If that does not happen it can be very painful. Most of the sibling rivalry I have seen can make a child doubt their sibling likes them let alone love them.

Once again, I searched the Word of God for any clue that sibling rivalry is normal. Just like the rebellion myth, I could not find anything in Scripture to support this lie. You see, the first time the Lord brings up brother treating brother with contempt, it was so heinous to God that He issued one of the most severe punishments recorded. I am referring to Cain. In Genesis chapter 4, we have the story of Cain and Abel, two brothers who had such a severe rivalry for Daddy God's attention that Cain ended up killing Abel out of jealousy. The result was Cain was driven from the two things he loved. First, he was driven from the presence of God, and second, he was driven from the land he loved to work. As it states in Genesis 4:13-14, "Cain said to the Lord, 'My punishment is more than I can bear. Today you are driving me from the land and I will be hidden from Your presence.'" The Bible goes on to say God put a mark on Cain so no one who found him would kill him. It appears God wanted Cain to feel the pain of what he had done for a very long time. This story tells me that God does not view sibling rivalry as a normal thing.

In the New Testament, God begins to refer to us, His children, as brothers and sisters in Christ. He goes on to tell us repeatedly that we are not to quarrel or fight but to love each other so completely that we would lay our lives down for each other. When Christ was asked what the greatest command was, His reply was to first love God with all our heart, mind, soul, and strength, then to love our brothers and sisters as ourself.

When children are born, they are born naturally selfish and their sin nature is very much at work. They have to be trained to love someone else, especially that brother or sister who also gets Mom and Dad's love and attention. As parents, we don't always know what is going on in their little heads, but I can tell you it normally doesn't flow toward selflessness. When Michael was a baby, Amy got sick, as older siblings often do. She would get in Michael's face, so I kept telling her to stay away from the baby because she was going to give him her cold. She continued to get in his face. When I told her again to stay away, she finally said, "But, Mommy, if I give it to him, doesn't that mean I won't have it anymore?" The heart she revealed in that moment is probably more prevalent in all of us than we care to admit. The only thing that changes that heart of selfishness is Jesus. So, until our children are saved and beyond, we, as their parents, are responsible to train them in the importance of loving their siblings.

Our homes are the best training ground we have to prepare our children for how God desires for them to live in the world they will encounter. If we do not train them to love, to sacrifice for, and to encourage their own siblings, how can we expect them to do that for the child sitting next to them in class? It will not just come naturally, especially if they are allowed to behave differently at home.

Our homes need to be the place where our children are safe to discover the gifts and calling God has placed on them. Just like when they learn to walk or ride a bike, they may have several failed attempts, so they need to know if they fall, we will pick them up and dust them off and say, "Let's try again." However, the best encouraging efforts of a parent can be completely destroyed by a jealous sibling. Now, if children could understand that their sibling is doing these things because they are jealous, it might change its intended effect, but unfortunately, most children have already listened to Satan tell them they lack value. All they are able to hear is their sibling saying, "You are not, and never will be, good enough." The truth is if we heard any other child say these things to our precious children that we are allowing their own brother or sister to get away with, we would be furious. We might even start an "end bullying campaign" at their school. Dare I go so far as to say that some of our school yard bullies learn their behavior from being allowed to treat their siblings that way at home. (They had to learn it somewhere.) I must also say that when a behavior at home goes unconfronted, it is the same thing as applauding that behavior and encouraging it to grow.

I know I am very passionate about this subject and I do not want to condemn anyone here, but if you realize you have been allowing this kind of behavior, it is never too late to do something about it. First, repent. Repent to Daddy God, and then, very importantly, repent to your children. Make the changes necessary to make your home a place for each and every child to flourish into who God called them to be.

Practically, one sign that one of your children may be being treated badly by a sibling is when they stop talking in family conversations due to fear of retribution or humiliation for what they have said. Another thing I can promise is that if you have heard your children say inappropriate comments to their sibling in front of you, I can guarantee that what is being said in private is ten times worse. Confront it. One thing I use to tell my children from a young age is

"You do not have permission to treat your brother or sister that way, and if you do, you have disobeyed me." I would explain how both Mommy and Daddy, along with God, will not allow them to treat anyone like that, especially their sibling. I would also explain how somebody I loved very much (the particular child) was hurting somebody else I loved very much (the sibling) and how that not only breaks my heart, but God's too because He made us to love each other.

Now, there are a lot of different types of corrections and punishments to stop this type of behavior, and I have used several of them. Ask God what will work best for your children. One punishment Amy and Michael still talk about it to this day is the unmatched sock basket. Like every house, we had a laundry basket full of unmatched socks. If I caught Amy and Michael fighting, they had to sit on the spare bed and try to find matches, and continue to do it until they stopped fighting. Without fail, before long, I would hear them laughing and getting along fine. Another thing I would have them do is come up with two or three things they admired about each other and tell each other these things face to face. Having them pray for each other was also very powerful. As they got older, they found it was hard to tear down someone you are praying for regularly. Frequently, I would have heart-to-heart talks with the older sibling about how much the younger sibling looked up to them, and how that gave them the responsibility to help the younger by looking out for them and encouraging him or her.

One day, I heard a friend of ours named Tom tell a story about his oldest son, Daniel, that captures the heart of this topic. He and Daniel were talking and Daniel felt like he was called to be a pastor someday. When Tom asked Daniel what he could do today to prepare himself for this role, Daniel said he could start by being a pastor to his younger brothers. I love it! We do not always have everything our children need. Sometimes one of their siblings might be the one who holds the key to breakthrough.

As an example, let me share this story. Our youngest son, Joseph, has dysgraphia and in kindergarten a high school student was assisting in teaching reading to his class. She somehow did something that led Joe to believe he could not read well. Jerry and I tried almost everything we could think of to get him to like reading because we knew how helpful it would be for him, but nothing seemed to click. Now, his big sister, Amy, has always has the gift of a teacher. One summer she developed a plan using her little brother's competitiveness to get him reading. She, all on her own, came up with a contest for him to win prizes for the amount of books he read over the summer. They would go to the library together and pick out books. With her own money, she even bought the prizes. She held a key for her brother that was so important for his life.

Likewise in our home, Michael has always been the one called to have the microphone, preaching and leading. From the time he was little, prophet after prophet visiting our church would call him out to give him a prophetic word. Joe has an incredible gift to encourage people to be the best they can be. Every time Michael would be called up front to be prophesied over, Joe would be front and center, phone in hand, recording every word. Michael also tends to be super hard on himself, and even though I tried to always be his cheerleader, it was Joseph who often reminded him of the words of God over his life. Someday Jerry and I won't be here anymore, but I can tell you that Amy, Michael, and Joseph have each other's backs. They are best friends. I will tell you the way they love each other is one of the ways their lives have honored Jerry and me. It has been a loud witness to non-Christians, because believe me, it is different from the world, and people notice that difference.

I believe Jesus has called our families to be light to a very dark world. For us to be light to darkness, we cannot embrace any of the lies Satan has inflicted on this world. Teenage rebellion and sibling rivalry are two that God really placed on my heart to call out for the evil they are. If something does not hold true to the Word of God, we must stand with God's living word. It is truth. It is our standard. If something doesn't sit right with you, pray about it. Take it to the Word of God to see if it is supported by scripture. If it fails these tests, I don't care who tells you it is normal or how long our culture has accepted the lie, do not let the enemy fool you too. Fight for truth for your family and the families in your church. God gave us a manual to live by and an open invitation to His throne room. He also tells us in 2 Corinthians 10:5, "We demolish arguments and every pretension that sets itself up against the knowledge of God, and we take captive every thought to make it obedient to Christ."

JERRY

At the root of sibling rivalry is the question of value. Who is the most important? Who is better? Every person, especially a child, wants to know that someone notices them and that they are special enough to receive unique attention. Left to our own devices, we will find a way to either make ourselves look better or attempt to make others look deficient. Unhindered flesh will find ways to use others to improve its standing and gain an edge in the competition for attention and value. As a father, if I notice rivalry among my children, it reveals to me that one, or all of them, does not feel valued. Like with Cain and Abel, it is a statement that "Your actions made me look bad, so I am going to eliminate you." We need to be diligent to maintain and be aware of the status of each child's "value meter": How self-secure and stable do your children feel? Is something going on in their lives (at home, school, friends, activities, sports, etc.) that makes them feel like they are failing? How can I reassure them and reinstate their understanding of their value?

When I was growing up, my brothers were not my rivals, but they were my competition. What is the difference you ask? At the heart, not much. On the surface, I knew openly degrading my older brothers would result in unpleasant consequences from them and my parents. But, if I could beat them at something, then I achieved the same purpose without opening myself to rebuke and would receive praise for my accomplishment. As long as I was "winning," I felt like I was valuable. If I was better than someone else, I was more esteemed. In our house, there was enough give-and-take that it equaled out and did not appear harmful. It actually became a love language of sorts. If my brother challenged me at something, it meant he respected my abilities enough that winning meant something. Unfortunately, the rest of the world did not always interact with me in that manner. When I challenged someone as an invitation to a relationship, most of the time they either recoiled, attacked violently, or, depending on the outcome, gloated or sulked. Not to mention, if they beat me, I felt horrible and worthless. There were only a few healthy relationships that started and continued in this manner.

As rivalry is based on value perception, comparison is the best way to determine value in a rivalry. One thing is evaluated against another to determine which I think is most beneficial for me. In our flesh, we compete and fight for a way to feel more valuable by trying to influence the comparison of us against others. That's how our kids are looking at each other until we intervene and show them the more perfect way.

Be aware that inherent value and practical abilities are two different things and must not be used interchangeably. Inherent value is the value God gave each of us. He looked over all of humanity and said, "Each one of you is worth the life of My Son." Everyone is equal in their inherent value. In God's eye, no one individual is worth more than another. Practical abilities are our gifts, talents, and skills that can be useful in various situations. If you are having problems with your central air conditioning, don't call me because I am nearly worthless. If you need someone knowledgeable in heating and air, call my friend John. He can help you. If you are having a medical issue, asking John would be unwise. But, if you asked me, I could assist you being a physician. I am as worthless in heating and air as John is worthless in medical issues, yet John and I are equal in the eyes of God, regardless of our abilities. John and I can both be confident that we are valuable to God and can relate to each other without feeling threatened or belittled. Likewise, we have to reassure our children that even though they cannot do something their sibling or friend is able to do that does not change how valuable they are to us or to God. God has granted them different gifts, and it takes patience and persistence to find those gifts. They can celebrate their sibling or friend's talent and not feel less valuable.

Additionally, comparison has to be used carefully. Because it is so easy to confuse inherent value and practical abilities, contrasting one child's efforts against those of their peers or siblings can be perceived as an evaluation of them in total. Your children may not understand the difference between value and abilities; all they may feel is the weight of comparison. A simple poem written by me illustrates this point:

Beware of comparison as a measurement of success,

For it resembles the rose.

Its fragrance can validate and affirm.

Its beauty can motivate and inspire.

Its thorns can cripple and condemn.

The ability to enjoy others' accomplishments and talents has fragrance and beauty, which can enlighten our life. However, if in order to be valuable we use their accomplishments as the standard for success, we risk the danger of condemning ourselves unnecessarily. In fact, if we can get our children to appreciate the blessing God has given their sibling or friend, they will approach what Jesus was trying to teach His disciples in Matthew 20:21-28 and Mark 10:35-45.

In these passages, James, John, and their mother approach Jesus to ask Him to grant the two brothers a place of honor. (Mark records that James and John went to Jesus with their request, while Matthew states their mother was the one who approached Jesus.) The other disciples were indignant when they found out. This was a question of who was the most important. No one wanted to be lower than the others. The questions came: "Who's the greatest?" "Which one of us is more valuable to You?" Jesus turned it upside down and corrected their understanding of God's standards. The greatest is not the one who is dominant or powerful. In God's kingdom, the servant is the most valuable; he resembles Jesus's life by giving and serving. In contrast to the world, being able to lord over others does not increase our value. To extend it a bit further, the ability to win or to come out on top does not increase one's value in the kingdom. In fact, it appears that Jesus says the opposite. The one who orchestrates his world so that others serve and cower before him is in danger of being in opposition to kingdom value. The servant, the one who gives away his life and abandons his pursuit of selfish superiority is the one who understands how to excel in the kingdom.

Understanding that value is at the root of rivalry and aggressively reinforcing to each child that he or she has value regardless of their abilities establishes a confidence that promotes love. If we can teach our kids these principles, and demonstrate it in how we interact with them and others, we will have gutted the monster of sibling rivalry.

SECTION TWO

This section is called seeking God's help. The reason we have titled it that is because our next point is that since God created your children, He is the only one who has the instruction manual. He is just waiting for you to come and ask him for it. This section contains chapters we believe will help you in your adventure of raising the gifts God has given to you.

CHAPTER 11

GO TO THE THRONE ROOM

DEBBIE

James tells us if we lack wisdom, we should ask our generous God and He will give it to us. I love that picture of God: generous. When it came to raising my children, I really needed a generous God. I sometimes look back at my life and I definitely regret some of the things I've done, but one thing I know I did right was to seek God about what to do for my children. I really knew in my heart that the lover of my soul was also the one who loved my children even more passionately than I did. When I couldn't understand the brain of a five-year-old boy, I knew God did. After all, He created my children and, as unique as they individually are, they have never been a puzzle to Him.

Now, it's occurred to me that often in the Christian world we use "Christian speak" and that not everyone reading this book will understand it. When I have said, "Go to the throne room," I fear some of you might be shaking your head in confusion. Well, the Bible refers to God's dwelling place as His throne room. In Philippians 4:8, the Bible tells us not to worry about anything but to take every situation to God in prayer and He will answer us. So when I'm speaking of going to the throne room, simply put, I'm saying talk to God. He created each of our children so we must consult him to understand his design in each of them.

The Bible tells me in Matthew 10:30 and Luke 12:7 that God even knows the number of hairs on my head. If He keeps track of the number of hairs on my head and on yours, then that tells me no detail of my life, or my child's life, is too small for Him. We really do have a God who wants to be intimately involved in every detail of our lives. He is not a Sunday morning God, so I should not be just a Sunday morning child.

Ephesians 3:12 says, "In Him (Jesus) we may approach God with freedom and confidence." Sometimes when I dwell on this, it is more mind blowing for me than I can put into words. We serve the creator of the whole universe, not just our planet, which is amazing in itself, but it is such a vast, vast universe. The universe is bigger and broader than we can understand or completely comprehend. Yet that amazing, and even sometimes terrifying, creator wants me to freely, and with confidence, approach Him. Even more amazing than that, the Bible tells me that as His child He will speak to me. Wow! The Bible sometimes refers to God as a shepherd and to us as His sheep whom He loves. In John 10:27, the Bible tells me that as His sheep, I can listen and know His voice. In verse 28, it goes on to say no one can snatch me out of His hand. These promises are true for your children too.

Now back to John 10:27 where the Bible says I can listen and know His voice. There are volumes of books written on the many ways we can hear the voice of God, and I am not going to even attempt to go through them in this chapter. But what I will say is God speaks. Our job is to seek Him out, ask Him our questions, and listen. For me, God has spoken through Scripture, pictures I envision, a voice I hear in my spirit that I have learned is His voice, and even the occasional dream. How He speaks to you may be different than it is for me. All I know is the Bible says He speaks and, as His sheep/children, we will know His voice. One clarification I will make is that He will never tell you to do something contrary to the Bible. So if you think He is telling you something that doesn't line up with Scripture, it is not Him. I recommend you talk with your pastor or spiritual mentor so they can help you learn to hear His voice. But one thing I'm sure of is that a great big God who can create a vast, mind-blowing universe can speak and be heard.

Even more amazing is that God wants a relationship with all of his children. I know that in every relationship I have ever had communication has been a two-way street. It wouldn't be much of a relationship if all that ever happened when I spent time with my friend was for me to talk the whole time and never expect him or her to respond. I'm pretty sure my friend would want me to shut up and listen every once in a while. God is no different. The Bible makes it clear that He wants us to know Him. For me, that meant I had to spend time where I shut up and listened. Romans 1:19-20 says that people are without excuse when it comes to God because He has made Himself known, even in the creation itself. God wants people to know Him so much He made His power and qualities known in His creation.

Whenever I learn more about God's creation, I am so aware of how amazing the God we follow is. From the creativeness that thinks of an animal like a giraffe, with its long neck, and the lion with its fierceness, to the many, many different and unique animal on our planet Gods amazing diversity is evident. Then there is the intricate coding in each tiny DNA strand that gives every living thing its unique qualities. I encourage you to slow down and take time to watch the sunset or look at how different each flower is. He says you will see the evidence of Him there. Then find someplace silent and listen. I promise He is there, and He wants you to know and hear Him. This amazing creator is just waiting for you, and I to go running to His throne and say, "Speak God, your servant is listening."

Going to the throne room in prayer is an absolute must when raising children. God is our ultimate source of wisdom and the creativity that we need to be successful in every pursuit. Every time I felt stuck or overwhelmed He had the breakthrough for each situation. Every good principle we used to raise our children came from the Word of God and prayer. He was always faithful to speak when I asked and He will do the same for you.

JERRY

I grew up in conservative, traditional, mainline, evangelical church environment. I had never heard of "going to the throne room." My perspective was "God is up in heaven and He will help me, if I'm good." If I really needed His help to get out of a jam, I thought He checked His schedule to see if He could find time to help me. Even with this erroneous mindset, He worked above my ignorance and found a way to lead me. I wasn't aware I could have such intimacy. Seeing myself sitting in His throne room and talking was never a consideration. I knew He would lead me, and He did lead me, even though I was clueless of how the process worked. I never doubted God's interest in me, I just did not think He and I could be that close. So I set myself to knowing God as best I could so I could fit in with His will. This meant learning the Bible. As I made decisions, I would compare them to the principles of the Bible and evaluate them on their consistency. He is the Truth, and if I wanted to know the best thing to do, then the Bible was the source. In coming to know His Word, I was having my mind renewed by the Spirit of God, even when my understanding of spiritual things was miniscule.

I was well into adulthood before I recognized the sound of that still, small voice and that the Helper was bringing to my remembrance what Jesus had said. Through His gentleness and life-changing love, I realized I did not have to send Him spiritual snail-mail and wait for His letter of response. I could have a living room conversation with Him. Praying continually does not mean I robotically go over my prayer list all day long. It means there is no reason I can't be in constant communication with Him. I can admit my weakness and inability and rely on Him for provision. I do not have to make myself rejoice all day long or force myself into thankfulness, I can live there. His will for me through Christ is that I can have an intimate, with-Him-all-day-long relationship. My personal interactions with God have become conversations, and frequently we communicate through Scripture.

In order to go to the throne room for my children, I had to become comfortable with God. Understanding the Bible is paramount. Humility is an absolute necessity. Willingness to listen and obey are the beginning place. As I developed a healthy relationship with God, I began to see His hand moving and was able to rejoice and be thankful, which opened the door for me to request His guidance. So even when I was unaware of His voice in my spirit, I followed what resonated His character. As I began to recognize His voice, it always sounded like Scripture. So if you are like I was and the active voice of God seems strange, at least dedicate yourself to knowing the Scripture so you can know His heart. If you do actively hear the voice of God and experience that type of relationship with Him, dedicate yourself to knowing the Scripture so you and the Holy Spirit have a common language and reference points. The passage to the throne room is revealed through an intense dedication to understand the Bible.

It starts with acknowledging that you need to be in the throne room. With the plethora of books on child rearing, it would be easy to focus on those works rather than trying to extract from a dusty, old Bible something that pertains to parenting. The experts speak clearly and definitively, but we must be diligent to filter what they say through what God is saying. The expert on your child and your ability as a parent is God. He will bring guidance through a friend's advice, a popular book, the Scripture, a podcast, or His still, small voice in your spirit. What is important is having an intimate and real relationship with Him so you know what to keep and what to throw away. Because each child is unique, one specific technique that works with one child may not work with another. God will give you what each child needs; we need merely ask and listen.

Since the throne room experience is essentially a relationship with open communication, you need to spend time with God. Time with Him does not require laying prostrate on the floor for an hour every morning before dawn. There may be a season for that, or it might be your thing, or it might never happen, but you, at the least, need to emotionally and mentally take that posture if you want to connect with the Lord. Biblical phrases like these can direct your attitude.

- "Be still, and know that I am God" (Ps. 46:10 ESV).
- "If my people who are called by my name humble themselves, and pray and seek my face and turn from their wicked ways, then I will hear from heaven and will forgive their sin and heal their land" (2 Chron. 7:14 ESV).
- "And when you pray, do not heap up empty phrases as the Gentiles do, for they think that they will be heard for their many words. Do not be like them, for your Father knows what you need before you ask him. Pray then like this, "Our Father in heaven, hallowed be your name.... (Matt. 6:7-9 ESV).

As Debbie mentioned, the Bible encourages His people to come to Him with confidence. Confidence that knows He hears, that He cares, and that He will do what is best. I have had to allow myself to be trained to not focus on what I want to happen but seek intently for what He wants to do. I have had to learn to distinguish between a pride that confidently expects Him to do what I have prayed for and a humility that lays my requests before Him, knowing He is well able, and being content with His actions. Many times I stopped praying because I thought He wasn't paying attention. I have since learned it was I who was not paying attention.

Going to the throne room for your children will involve moments of weeping alone in the dark, crying out for His mercy, grace, and guidance. It will also deliver moments of gratitude as you see Him moving the impossible mountain of a toddler's will or a teenager's attitude. Included as well will be the pause to quickly ask for patience and wisdom as you react to your child's behavior. I encourage you and your spouse to frequently set aside time together to pray for each child. Do not do so only when the kids are in a mess and you need guidance for a way out but also when things are runny smoothly. The mindset you have when coming to God will affect how you pray, what you pray for, and how you hear. Don't stop praying, regardless if your children are doing well or doing poorly. Heed Paul's words to pray without ceasing (1 Thess. 5:17) and follow the example of his prayers (Eph. 1:15-19, 3:14-19; Phil. 1:3-11; Col. 1:3-5, 9-14).

If something is not clear, be patient, and don't expect to get the same type of information for each child. We knew before age two what Michael's call was. It proved to be very valuable as we guided him into opportunities and through hard times. For Joe, all I got when I asked God about his future was, "Keep him between the ditches, by the time he's a teenager, it will all come together." I would go back to God and ask for more guidance for Joe. I was afraid we were going to miss something and shipwreck him since we didn't have the same clarity for him that we had for the other two . But as we watched their personalities develop, keeping Michael tied to the ground so he didn't run off into the sunset prematurely and patiently watering Joe with the Word and love, the wisdom in how God managed us managing them was revealed. Joe needed what he got, and Michael needed what he got. My demand for equality only made things confusing for them and me.

While you are in the throne room beseeching God to bring your child through a tough season, don't become so distracted by the splinter in your child's eye that you miss the log sticking out of yours. More times than I care to admit, I was carrying the same wrong attitude that my child was displaying. I was prolonging these seasons of discord because of sin that needed to be dealt with in me. Sometimes weeks would go by with the problem persisting. Hundreds of episodes of behavior correction and attitude adjustment, but nothing would change. That rebellious, unsubmitted, wayward child was continuing in a behavior and attitude that was destroying the whole house. I would be approaching the point of explosion when God would hold the mirror up so I could see the plank in my eye. Sometimes gently, most of the time rather bluntly, He would sit me down like I had been setting my rebellious child down, look me in the eye, and lay out what was happening. After crying and repenting to God, I would repent to my wife and the children, and set a path of correction for me and them. We would all go to visit the throne room. Soon, the spiritual atmosphere in my house would change. (Warning: If there is a bad atmosphere in your house, don't forget to look in the mirror before attacking everyone else. Dads, this is on us. The throne room experience provides the opportunity for God to rearrange us so we can arrange our house. Share the mercy that was given to you.)

With that being said, your kids don't get a free pass because you're a spiritual idiot. My goal was to mentor my children using correction and example. They needed to see and experience the impact of the throne room. They needed to receive what God gave me for them, plus I needed to show them how to go there themselves. There they can expect to get words for themselves and others.

When it comes to raising children the best starting place, final destination, and everything in between is in the throne room. Live there. Abide in Him. Soak up His wisdom. Seek and obey His guidance. And show your kids how to do the same.

CHAPTER 12
PRAY WITHOUT CEASING

DEBBIE

First Thessalonians 5:16 says, "Rejoice always, pray continually, and give thanks in all circumstances for this is God's will for you in Christ Jesus." Give thanks in all circumstances? Now, this idea can be overwhelming to think about. As Americans, we are definitely not taught to give thanks in all circumstances. Just take a small glance at Facebook and you will quickly see that most of us need some work when it comes to thankfulness. I'm sure that goes for the rejoicing and continual prayer too. Hebrews 4:15 says our high priest, Jesus, can empathize with our weaknesses because He was tempted in every way, just like us. Because of this, Jesus understands what you and I deal with being human. Somehow, though, He was able to conquer sin. That is encouraging. I don't have to be someone who stands on my right to express my every grievance. I can have a heart that lives in thankfulness.

To me, God doesn't put these three things together by accident: rejoicing, continual prayer, and thankfulness. He has really been showing me the importance of thankfulness lately. I was having a conversation with one of my friends named Michelle the other day and she shared a quote I truly love. Though I can't remember the original source, the quote is, "All things are sanctified through thanksgiving."

You see, Romans 8:28 says, "And we know that in all things God works for the good of those who love Him, who have been called according to His purpose." If I believe God will work everything (and I mean everything) out for my good, then when I thank Him for everything, His presence will invade every situation. When His presence shows up, there will be sanctification. When I thank Him, He is there. In the act of thanksgiving, I am recognizing His presence, which means praying, and I can recognize He is working on my behalf so I can rejoice.

Philippians 4:6 says, "Do not be anxious about anything, but in every situation by prayer and petition with thanksgiving present your requests to God." For so many years, I've quoted this verse this way: "Do not worry but in every situation present your requests to God." I was completely missing the point. We cannot leave out thanksgiving. If I don't thank God for the last revelation He gave me or the last time He answered my request, I am missing out on that burst of faith that reminds me of His repeated faithfulness which makes worrying unnecessary because God has everything under His control. Not to mention, if I forget to thank Him for all He has done, could I be so rude as to ask Him for more? My daughter challenged me with a quote she heard: "Tomorrow when we wake up, if all we had left was what we remembered to thank God for today, what would that be?" I'm determined not to be convicted by that quote again. I want to be grateful in all situations.

When Michael was a little more than one, he was one of the most determined little guys I've ever seen. If he set his mind on something, the old distract-him-thing never worked. I was growing frustrated because I felt like I was just saying, "No," and spanking his little hand all day long. Then I was putting Amy to bed one night and as she was saying her prayers she began to pray that God would help Michael to not get into trouble tomorrow. I was so convicted because I realized I had not been praying for God to help him. I know when my children were little it was so easy to be overwhelmed by the business of life and to forget to pray continually. I now realize I not only should have been praying for God to help him, but I should have stopped in every situation and asked God to come and help him in the moment AND (very important) thanked God.

JERRY

Praying without ceasing has several applications. It can involve constantly thinking and verbalizing praise, thankfulness, and requests as we move through our day. Another form encourages us to never stop praying until we have received our request , as promoted in Luke 11:5-13. Daniel demonstrates another way to pray without ceasing. In Daniel 6:10, we see two things about Daniel's prayer life. First, he had an established routine he fulfilled every day. Second, regardless of the consequences, he continued that routine. Nothing could thwart this communion with God. I have also heard that since prayer is a reflection of our submission to God (we need His help, we acknowledge His greatness, we ask for His will to be done and not ours, we repent when not following His standards, etc.), a life that reflects that submission in every word and deed is a prayer; a prayer that never ceases, until we refuse to submit.

As I have grown, I have wrestled with this concept. Which view is correct? Is there another view that explains it better? My current answer is "Yes." Yes to all of the above.

When you are serious about your relationship with God, you probably have functioned, and continue to function, according to all of these views. The thing that has led me to be a pray-without-ceasing person is my desire to be with God. I have sought to emulate Daniel in his understanding that God is so wonderful, how could he not spend time revering and honoring Him regardless of what was going on? Jesus invites us to become dependent upon God for everything. Will not the Father give good gifts to His children? I have wasted most of my life trying to prove to God I was independent and didn't need Him to take care of me. That's pretty close to what happened in the Garden of Eden. It reeks of arrogance and pride. But the Father invites us to come to Him for everything.

JERRY AND DEBBIE BURBEE

> ¹² If I were hungry, I would not tell you,
> for the world and its fullness are mine.
> ¹³ Do I eat the flesh of bulls
> or drink the blood of goats?
> ¹⁴ Offer to God a sacrifice of thanksgiving,
> and perform your vows to the Most High,
> ¹⁵ and call upon me in the day of trouble;
> I will deliver you, and you shall glorify me.
> Psalms 50:12-15 ESV

This passage reminds us that He does not need us to feed Him. We may think our sacrifices provide Him with something, but actually, He is the only one who is self-sufficient. In verse 14, He encourages us to be thankful of what He has done and to remain faithful to our commitment to Him. This awareness of Him, combined with verse 15, captures the life cycle of a child of God.

1. I am thankful for what He has done.
2. I am committed to honoring His character.
3. I am dependent upon Him for help in my everyday life.
4. He hears, provides, and delivers.
5. I acknowledge His mercy and love and proclaim His goodness.
6. (Return to step one.)

Psalm 66 echoes these thoughts:

> Come and listen, all you who fear God,
> and I will tell you what he did for me.
> For I cried out to him for help,
> praising him as I spoke.
> If I had not confessed the sin in my heart,
> the Lord would not have listened.
> But God did listen!
> He paid attention to my prayer.
> Praise God, who did not ignore my prayer
> or withdraw his unfailing love from me.

(Psalms 66:16-20 NLT)

Let's look at what the psalm writer says:

1. He respects God.
2. He proclaims what God has done.
3. He cried out for help.
4. He praised Him in the midst of his trial.
5. He repented.
6. God listened.
7. He praises God.
8. He enjoys God's love.

Both of these passages reveal the essence of praying without ceasing and support the views given above.

1. My mind is centered on Him and that is what I think and speak.
2. I am confident God will hear me and I pursue Him so I can enjoy His love.
3. Regardless of the circumstances, I dwell with Him and will shape my day for those purposes.
4. My life will be one of repentance and commitment as I honor Him with all that I do.

In full disclosure, living my life this way has been a process and not an achievement. Every day contains success and disappointment. Every day involves experiencing the fullness of this experience and the frustration of having come up short part of the time. Thankfully, His mercy is new every morning, and I can set out for it again.

In relation to child rearing, this is at the core of our parenting abilities. Recall the old saying "Kids learn more from watching how you live, rather from you telling them how to live." A life of gratitude and submission is felt and absorbed. Understanding how to navigate hard times is best learned from a shared experience. When we live a life of unceasing prayer, and share with our kids the life we have with God, they will see and touch what is possible.

In respect to actual prayers I have prayed, the constant prayer for my children to have a relationship with Him always echoes through my soul:

"Father, that they would see You as You are. That they would find an even deeper place in You than I have known. That You would come to them and reveal Yourself so that they know You personally."

As challenges and problems surface, all day long I am lifting them up for His guidance. Debbie and I return to ask that He show them their place in His kingdom and how we can help. We frequently repent and ask God to reveal where we need further repentance, while also asking that repentance be granted to them as needed. Our desire is to always praise and thank God for all that He is doing, has done, and will do.

Praying without ceasing is not a command Paul threw in at the end of 1 Thessalonians just to lay another burden on the people of God.

> *Always be joyful. Never stop praying. Be thankful in all circumstances,* ***for this is God's will for you who belong to Christ Jesus.***

> *(1 Thessalonians 5:16-18 NLT)*
> *(emphasis mine)*

Paul was not demanding that we shape up and get our act together. He was reminding us of what is now available since we belong to Jesus. We don't have to conjure up the moxy to make it happen; it is God's will for us to have this type of access to Him. All day long we can be in communication with the Creator of the Universe. We can be joyful and thankful, no matter what is going on. God's will is done on earth as it is in heaven, and that includes us getting to tap into the power of transformation which releases us to participate in a relationship with the Father similar to the one Jesus has. We don't **have to** live this way; we **get to** live this way. We don't have to raise our children to know this; we get to. What a pleasure it is to see that fruit.

CHAPTER 13
THE BIBLE IS THE ULTIMATE TRUTH

DEBBIE

We live in a world where "truth" is under attack and even being redefined. In 2016, Oxford Dictionary named "post-truth" as its word of the year. Post-truth is an adjective defined as "relating to or denoting circumstances in which objective facts are less influential in shaping public opinion than appeals to emotion or personal belief." We have become a culture that says there is no ultimate truth. Therefore, what I think or feel is true is truth to me, aka "my truth," and what you think or feel is true to you, aka "your truth," but as far as an ultimate truth, there is none. That is a scary place to stand. Years ago in college, I took an ethics class and discovered you could create a strong argument for or against any subject if there was no standard defining right and wrong, like the Bible does, thus making ethics and morality subject to the situation, i.e. situational ethics. This mentality of choosing personal truth has even been creeping into the Church.

The Bible is the Holy Spirit-inspired word of God. It is not, and never will be, outdated because we now consider ourselves a more enlightened culture. No, it is either the inspired, completely true word of God or it is a worthless book. If we can begin to pick and choose which parts are true and which parts are not, then I would say the whole book must now be labeled as fiction. If I can determine certain

Biblical statements about behavior are not true, and it is therefore a mistake to call those behaviors a sin, then how can I believe that any other part of the Word is not also false? For example, did Jesus really rise from the dead?

We are on shaky ground, my friends, when we begin to decide what parts of the Bible, or of God Himself, we will choose to believe or not. Several theological disciplines, such as apologetics, textual criticism, historical criticism, and canonical criticism, study the Bible using history, archeology, and available portions of the original texts to prove our Bible is as close to the original text as possible. Several of the stories in the Bible are supported by historical data and archeological finds. There are volumes and volumes written on this subject, but for my purposes, I will only say that the Bible was so meticulously copied and preserved by the scribes that we have more original manuscripts of it than any other written work. We can prove our Bible is a more accurate text than any of Shakespeare's works, yet few people will throw out Romeo and Juliet because we cannot prove its validity. As far as science goes, I know a lot of Christians who fear it because they believe it will prove God's Word to be wrong. Not me. I'm a science geek and I love how, time and time again, science that counters Scripture is always proven wrong and God's Word stands. In fact, science itself has to break its own rules to try to make evolution a fact, there is no scientific experiment, or evidence, that can recreate any portion of evolution or support it.

All this is to say if God is the God the Bible says He is, then He can definitely protect and pass His words from one generation to another exactly as He wants them to survive. The fact is the Bible is the Holy Spirit-inspired, infallible word of God. God Himself tells us we are to know His words and teach them to our children. I would be remiss if I left out what the Bible itself tells us about its words. Second Timothy 3:16-17 says, "All Scripture is given by inspiration of God, and is profitable for doctrine, for reproof, for correction, for instruction in righteousness that the man of God may be complete, thoroughly equipped for every good work." The Greek word for inspiration used here literally means "God-breathed." So you see, the Bible itself tells us that it is the literal words of God Himself. Yes, it was written down by men, but it was God who gave them the words to write. Second Peter 1:2 confirms this statement saying, "Above all, you must understand that no prophesy of Scripture came about by the prophets own interpretation of things...Spoken from God as they were carried along by the Holy Spirit." Psalms 12:6 adds: "And the words of the Lord are flawless like silver purified in a crucible, like gold refined." Proverbs 30:5 repeats this idea when it states, "Every word of God is flawless.," and Psalms 119:89 records, "Heaven and earth will pass away, but my words will never pass away." James 1:22 follows all this up by telling us we are not just supposed to know His words, we are to live them: "Do not merely listen to the words and so deceive yourself, do what it says."

God did not give us our Bible as a book to be enjoyed as a good fictional story. It is His very words. We are to learn from it, but not just learn from it or to memorize it, but to do what it says. The Bible must remain our ultimate source of truth. The Bible itself says it stands eternal. Our feelings and our science will constantly change, but the Word of the Lord will remain forever. It will stand when everything else falls. We can put our faith in it, believe it, teach it, and more importantly, do what it says as we teach our children to do the same.

JERRY

The urge in our modern culture to redefine our standards started with valid questions about equality, racism, and tradition which brought needed changes and necessary conversation, filling the twentieth century with discussions about our humanity as we engaged world wars, the Cold War, riots, and protests and with questions concerning the legitimacy of the old standards. As the traditions and presuppositions were challenged, an unasked question lingered in the background: "Are there any standards of the past that should not be challenged?" Here is where our society is split. Many proclaim that all past rules and expectations need to be abolished and new standards better reflecting the reality of modern civilization need to be developed while others assert that if certain principles are eliminated, our modern community will dissolve into chaos. Even if there is agreement that some things must remain, there is no consensus on which ones to leave in place. A cursory review of history reveals this dilemma is common to the cycles of social order; what standards are to be used to govern our society? As parents, we must challenge ourselves to determine which factors are influencing our standards and morals.

In Genesis 3:10-11, Adam tells God he was hiding because he was naked, to which God replies, "Who told you were naked?" The course of events began with Eve listening to the serpent, being swayed by his assertions, and deciding the fruit looked good, and since it promised wisdom, she ate. Adam was also convinced that the suggestions of the serpent and his personal insight were more substantial than God's command to not eat the fruit. Whose voice influenced Adam and Eve? Who told them they were naked? They decided that the serpent's reasoning and their own wisdom was valid justification to violate what God had decreed. The question is repeated to us today: "Whose voice are you listening to?" We must decide who has the wisdom and authority to establish standards. Are you secure that your own judgments are sufficient? Or the declarations of Hollywood's most successful star? Or the current wave of collective thought? Or the intellectuals? Or that which makes you the most comfortable? We choose what we will use for our standards and we also choose the source for those standards.

Whose voice are you listening to?

If we think God is the ultimate authority, how do we determine His standards? As Debbie laid out, the Bible presents itself as an all-or-nothing representation of God. If we reject part of the Bible, we are rejecting all of it, and rejecting God's ability to provide to us a reliable representation of Himself. Most who are reading this book would agree the Bible is trustworthy and the biggest challenge is in clarifying what exactly is being said. The challenge for us is not whether we agree with the voices of the world, but rather are we aware of how those voices influence how we read the Bible? These voices are the ones that encourage us to pick and choose what fits with these new standards, putting us at ease because we have found a way to have the Bible's approval. My advice is to prayerfully seek clarity on the core elements of the Bible's message, stand firm on those, and carefully evaluate new ideas against those core elements. As the process is engaged, carefully critique your susceptibility to the voices that influence you and the origin of those voices; not all input is helpful.

Another subpoint to this discussion is conviction. Are we willing to stand against opposition to our conclusions? Resistance may come from our children, our spouse, our extended family, our friends, our church, our community, and/or our government. Are we convinced that our verdict on the evidence is accurate and worth dying for? This statement seems extreme, but, in the small things, the big things find their power. We might not face a firing squad because we refuse to denounce Jesus publicly, but we will have to decide if our ten-year-old is mature enough to watch an R rated movie or the best way to answer our eight-year-old's question about gender choice. Refusing to acquiesce to pressure is necessary for things we know to be true, but are we also willing to abandon those conclusions that are not true in order to adopt truth? Again, how do we determine what is true? Is there an absolute truth?

In John 11 is the story of Jesus raising Lazarus from the dead. In seeing this miracle, some came to believe in Jesus (v 45), others went to the Pharisees (v 46), and there were those who already believed in Him (His disciples, Mary, Martha). Personally, I cannot imagine seeing someone raised from the dead and not being convinced that Jesus was the Messiah, but it seems that visible proof is not always convincing. I would conjecture that those who went to the Pharisees had already decided about who Jesus was and any evidence, such as raising the dead, only made Him more of a threat to their reality rather than being influential in rearranging their reality. The disciples had their conclusions confirmed, and those who newly believed were not sure until they saw the miracle. This story illustrates the human response to truth: "I have already decided and nothing can change my mind" or "If the new evidence fits with my previous truths, I can accept this new truth." We see what we want to see, but we can also be influenced by other factors.

The world labels Christians as blind followers because we have reached a conclusion that will not change—God is the origin of all truth, and despite the facts or inferences they fire in our direction, we do not move. Conversely, we have made the same accusation against many non-Christians. They can be as passionate about their convictions as we are, even willing to die for them. They degrade us for having a faith that is not rational and we charge them with arrogance and rebellion because they place their trust in themselves and the things they can touch. The core issue here: "Who can I trust?"

Trust is a major component of any relationship, and the level of trust regulates the level of intimacy and reliability of the connection. If I trust and that trust is rewarded with an appropriate response, I will be willing to trust again if something unknown or questionable arises. If the response to my trust does not meet my expectations, I will be less likely to extend that trust again. As Christians, our assertion is that we have the depth of relationship with God that affords us the ability to trust when things are unpredictable, and to trust even when the conclusion of an event does not meet our expectations. We echo Shadrach, Meshach, and Abednego who said, "If we are thrown into the blazing furnace, the God we serve is able to deliver us from it, and he will deliver us from Your Majesty's hand. But even if he does not, we want you to know, Your Majesty, that we will not serve your gods or worship the image of gold you have set up" (Dan. 3:17-18 NIV).

I know my God is able to do anything, but even if He does not do what I expect or want, I know Him well enough to know that He is smarter than me and His choice is the best. Therefore, I only listen to His voice.

To circle back around, we decide what we will trust as truth. Some will decide their truth is that there is no truth, except for what the individual wants to be true. Some will pick and choose tasty morsels from the buffet of prevailing theories. Some will cling to the Rock because He has proven Himself faithful. For most of us, the times we have difficulty holding the Bible as the absolute truth and living with that unwavering conviction comes because our relationship with Him is shallow and we do not have our own stories of how He has been faithful over and over. Since we do not know the depth of His nature, we do not trust He will have our best interest at heart and thus we look for alternatives. Truth and trust are yoked together like two oxen; if they are not unified, little successful work can be accomplished. As parents, the truth we transfer to our children shapes the course of their life, influences what they will accept and reject, and sets their reality.

What will we teach them?

Who do you trust to have the truth?

Who do you say that He is?

Which voice will you listen to?

CHAPTER 14
YOU NEED HELP

DEBBIE

When she was first lady, Hillary Clinton was credited with the phrase "It takes a village to raise a child." She understood that rarely does the individual family unit of mom, dad, and children have all that is needed to give a child everything he or she needs to be successful in this world. In our culture, it is not uncommon for children to grow up and leave the town and family where they were raised to pursue academic or career success. It wasn't always this way. As short as a few decades ago, families seemed to stay more central and it was common for grandparents, uncles, and aunts to remain in the same area, maybe even in the same house, providing support to the next generation. Hillary recognized how isolated families have become and how stressful it can be for a two-income family to care for the needs of their children. The problem was that Hillary called upon a mostly self-centered society to pull on their heart strings to band together for the sake of the children. That only works if people embrace a common goal and become selfless enough to reach out and give of themselves to see this happen. So now, not only does the overworked, stressed-out mom have her own full-time job and household to worry about, she is supposed to help raise her neighbors' kids too. Hillary was asking society to have the heart of Jesus and basically to become the Church.

In the Church, we have the common goal and the call from our Savior to lay down our lives for others to make this happen. If we are not, then I will say, we should be.

When my husband and I moved away from the families and town we had grown up in so Jerry could pursue his medical degree, the first thing we did was to find a body of believers we felt God was calling us to be a part of. To this day, I thank God profusely for taking us to Life Church in Kirksville, Missouri. My husband and I had been crying out to God for a body of believers who were serious about their pursuit of Him and lived a Christianity that consumed every part of their lives, not just Sundays, and maybe Wednesday nights too. At Life Church, we were able to connect to a people that had a passion for Jesus, and they became our people, the people we had been searching for.

We fell completely in love with the Church. These people truly believed the call of God to love the Lord God with all your heart, mind, soul, and strength, then secondly, to love your neighbor as yourself. They had a passion for legacy that did not stop with their individual families, but extended to the legacy of each and every family in the church.

The Bible gives each parent the mandate to raise and train their own children in the ways of God. Unfortunately in America, we have given that mandate over to the government. A government that in their pursuit of training children somehow felt you must separate church and state to do so in a way which eventually went to the extreme of taking church completely out of the government. I don't know about you, but I'm guessing like me, you do not share the same values that are proclaimed by our government anymore.

As a Church, we looked around and realized that no single individual has everything needed to train and educate our children, but together we could pool our resources and have just that. We truly held the value that if my children have their needs met, then yours should too. One for all and all for one. God had blessed His people in a way that our combined talents could not only educate our children, but do so with excellence in an environment that did not separate God from the equation, instead welcoming Him into every facet of it. So our church formed both a daycare and a school that went from four-year-old kindergarten through high school.

When Jerry and I began to have our children, one thing we did was look around our church and find a couple who had teenagers that were passionate for God; teenagers that looked like what we wanted our children to become. We went to that couple and basically said, " We know we are going to need help, so we want to submit ourselves to you. Please teach us from the things you have learned from God while raising your children." They were, and still remain, a wonderful source of wisdom for us in every new stage of parenting we encounter. Now, here comes the tough part: we even said, "If you see us doing something wrong, please, please come tell us." This sounds like a nice idea, but believe me it is not an American idea, and it is harder to walk out in real life than it sounds. Fortunately, they loved us enough to do that, and we humbled ourselves enough to listen when they did. Today, our children are full grown adults and have left our home, but we still glean from Wendell and Kathy's advice on parenting, and now how to be godly grandparents.

Side Note: This relationship only works if you are honest with yourself and the other couple when you need help. They committed to love and care about the welfare of our children. They paid attention to the interaction they were able to see us have with our children, but they are not omniscient like God. If we were struggling somewhere, many times we had to swallow our pride and go ask for their opinions, prayer, and advice. Also, if they observed something and felt they needed to come to us, we had to be humble, not take offense, and listen because if pride gets in the way, even the truth spoken in love can be hard to hear. They were patient and loving, and we are eternally grateful to them, and especially to God for bringing them into our lives. Also, please note that we went to them and asked for their discipleship. We opened the door for them. As that older adult, I now understand why Christ spoke to the crowds in stories and parables, but to His disciples He was able to speak more plainly. You can only speak into someone's life to the level they have allowed. So if you know you could benefit from some older couple's wisdom, go ask for it. Don't just wait around hoping someone will walk up and offer.

There were so many things our children needed that Jerry and I could not give them, but God was faithful to surround us with other Christians who could fill those needs. All of my children had calls to be worshippers. I could give them a heart for worship by sharing my passion for it, but I cannot play an instrument at all. Sandy and Ruth became perfect teachers for them to fill this void. Just recently, my husband and children all played together to provide worship for a wedding, and as I listened, God's faithfulness to that call of worship was so evident. People, we serve a good God!

There will come times when you are faced with choices of who will train your child in some aspect of life. You may feel like one person has more excellence in a particular area of training versus someone who may be simply adequate but not exceptional at the task but who shares the same passion for Jesus that you want to see in your child. Because I am a teacher, I can tell you every teacher not only teaches the information needed, but more importantly, each imparts who they are to their students, both good and bad. When I was faced with the choice of teachers to train my child, it was easy because I chose the person with a heart for Jesus. I knew my children would get the same knowledge from both teachers, but I did not have to worry about what the unsaved person might expose them to.

In the church, God provided grandparents, aunts and uncles, and a boat load of cousins for my children. That never lessened their love for their immediate family. In fact, because God had called Jerry ad I to serve Him in a place apart from our own family, it became a blessing to be a part of a church that loved my children like that. I can say for us as a church, we have taken the mandate to love our brother as ourselves completely to heart. That often means giving of our time and money to benefit other families. I became Momma Burbee to so many children, and I have found incredible joy in loving them like my own. I can also say many times my heart has been grieved and broken when one of these children was struggling or did not seem to be making it. I have poured my heart out to God for many hours of intercession over them. We have also opened our home to take some of them in when they were struggling. When we got the call that a child we loved was in need, we did not even hesitate to open our home and bring them in. I have even found myself walking into a drug house to pull someone out. The amazing thing we could count on was we knew their parents would do the same for our children if the situation was reversed. Our congregation has lived this principle of God so fully that in some situations, couples in our church have even agreed to assume guardianship for another family's children if something should happen to the parents.

I know not everyone reading this book is fortunate enough to be a part of a church like Life Church. I am confident, though, if you pray and ask God, He will lead you to others who long for fellowship with other believers who love the Lord like you do. I know for certain that God loves your children even more than you do and He will provide. In Matthew 19:29, after the rich, young ruler walked away sad because he could not give up his wealth to become Jesus's disciple, Jesus made a promise. In this promise, I believe Jesus is referring to the Church when He says, "And everyone who has left houses or brothers or sisters or fathers or mothers or wife or children or fields for My sake will receive a hundred times as much and will inherit eternal life." So, with a thankful heart for all God has already done in your life, bring your desires before Him, then watch what He will do. He is the God who provides – our Jehovah-jireh.

JERRY

Earlier in this book, Debbie and I told you that everything you needed to raise your kids, God would provide. We encouraged you to have the confidence to seek God and to act on what He guided you into. You are the ones to be your children's parents. Don't abdicate that role to the government, society, or your fears. You might wonder now how can we say, "You are going to need help"? As you may have concluded from Debbie's section, we consider them one and the same: God provides all that we need; sometimes it comes through others.

I am reminded of the story of the man who was stranded on top of his house during a flood. He prayed earnestly, full of faith, for God to come rescue him. The rain continued to fall, the waters continued to rise, and the soaked man waited in hope against all hope. Before long a good ole boy in his fishing boat came by and offered to take the man to safety. But the man did not waver in his faith and boldly proclaimed, "Thank you for your kindness, but I have prayed and asked God to rescue me and will wait here until He comes." Several minutes later, the soggy individual was greeted by a government rescue boat that was sweeping through the area to rescue the stranded. Again, the man declined and affirmed his faith in God coming to rescue him. As the rain subsided and the clouds cleared, the shivering man was greeted by a rescue helicopter to take him from the flood waters. Again, he stood his ground and waved the helicopter away. As the water continued to rise, and there was barely any space left on his roof, the man turned his face to the heavens and cried in desperation, "God, I prayed for deliverance. Did you not hear my earnest plea for help? Why have You not responded to my prayer?" The sky broke open, a gleam of light shot through the clouds, and God's voice boomed through the heavens like thunder. "I came three times, and each time you told Me to go away. What else do you want?"

This story reminds me of the importance of our humility to seek God's help and the wisdom to notice it when it comes. Like the man on the roof, I am sometimes insulted if God does not move in the amazing, movie-type miracle that stuns everyone and gives me a great tale to tell. My expectations are set; I know God can do it, and I have it all rehearsed in my mind exactly how it should go. During one of these periods of my life, I ran across 2 Kings 5. In this chapter, Naaman goes to Elisha expecting a miraculous healing and is insulted that he has come all this way to be told to wash himself in the nasty Jordan river. Fortunately, he listened to the wisdom of his servants. "Naaman's servants went to him and said, 'My father, if the prophet had told you to do some great thing, would you not have done it? How much more, then, when he tells you, 'Wash and be cleansed!'" (2 Kings 5:13 NIV). After Naaman obeyed, he was restored and had skin like a young boy.

The wisdom of God is essential to know how to navigate parenting. "How do I know what to discipline and what to encourage?" "How am I to help my child succeed?" And on and on the questions bombard us. We can have confidence that God will provide if we have the humility to ask and to receive it in the form He supplies. Humility involves making ourselves vulnerable to the judgement of others. As I have encountered families over the years, I am surprised at how few take advantage of the wise parenting advice that is so near. As Debbie mentioned, asking Wendell and Kathy for help seemed like the obvious thing to do, but I am puzzled why others hesitate to do the same. I think some hold back because they are so insecure in their parenting abilities that admitting to someone they need help would only confirm to them that they are near failures. Many will hesitate because they are not sure they can trust the counsel of an outsider. Others don't ask because they are completely assured that they are doing everything right. Then there are those who simply do not like being told what to do. As with everything human, fear and arrogance impede our abilities to find God's wisdom. We must continue to seek that balance between having the confidence that snuffs out fear and the humility that prevents arrogance from leading us blindly over a cliff. Waiting for someone to ask if we need help is convenient in that we do not have to be vulnerable in asking for help, and if no one offers, we are not responsible. How much moxy is required to present ourselves before someone and say, "Examine me, discover my flaws, then develop a training routine that will stretch me beyond what is comfortable and firmly guide me through the process, even if it involves suffering, to a better version of me?" From experience, I know I was not teachable until I amassed that amount of trust and made myself vulnerable. Placing myself in another person's hands seemed unnecessarily risky until I realized I was actually trusting God to move through that person, similarly to how He was sending rescuers to the man on the roof. If we are asking God for help, we need to recognize God when He comes, in whatever form He comes. So it is not moxy we need, it is faith in God.

Spiritual confidence and humility contrasted against the fleshly counterparts of fear and arrogance are a distinction we need to carefully consider. We shouldn't turn ourselves over to others as mindless minions but as friends, brothers, and sisters seeking God together for our children. "Without counsel plans fail, but with many advisers they succeed" (Prov. 15:22 ESV). Going to God for the wisdom to raise our children includes asking for the wisdom concerning whom else to involve in this process. We need mentors; our children need mentors. The only question to ask is "Who are those people?" Once God reveals His choice, we have to act wisely in engaging them. When that relationship is formed, and our mentors suggest a change that is not easy or comfortable, prayerfully consider what God would want before ignoring the advice. Humans make mistakes, but God knows that and accounts for it.

When selecting guides for your children, prayerfully consider the goals, the timing, and the individuals who will be influencing them. Preferably, you would want to choose people you know and trust, but occasionally, you may want to consider someone you don't know if that person offers something your friends cannot. In nearly every aspect of training and learning, those outside your circle of trusted individuals may be the next step in your child's development. Be careful. Seek out what others may know of this new person. Consider the maturity of your child.l. Does the child have the maturity to filter through any ungodly encounters that might occur? Can we be available to attend the rehearsal or practice so we see everything our child experiences? Will we take the time to debrief them on their encounters? Is the child going into a safe environment? As we do not know everything, we need discernment to plot our course.

Are you willing to admit you need help? Do you have the faith and the humility to trust another couple to teach you? Do you have the confidence to rely on God's faithfulness to guide you? As the water is rising and the flood is ready to sweep you away, will you accept the help God sends?

CHAPTER 15
YOUR RELATIONSHIP WITH THE FATHER

DEBBIE

If I were to ask you the question "Why are you here on this Earth?" I would hope your answer would have something to do with God and His plan for your life. For me, I never doubted the idea that there was a creator. When I looked at the world around me, I could not even entertain the thought that it all came from some big random accident. Nothing this amazing and intricate could ever exist without a creator. As a child, I even had a sense that somehow that creator wanted to be involved with me. I grew up in a Christian home and was part of a church that stressed knowing the Bible, so as a young person I studied it and had that childlike faith to believe if the Bible said something was true, then it was.

I know my story is not like everyone else's, but if you are reading this book I would think you would have stopped by now if you were not a believer. Due to the fact you are still reading, I will assume you are a Christian. There are many types of people in this day and age who call themselves Christian, and I have no desire to judge anyone's faith, but in this chapter we will be talking about your relationship with God the Father.

Jerry and I have said over and over that our parenting blueprint came from the Bible and that the best things we ever did as parents came from spending time in prayer and listening to the Holy Spirit. So for us, the relationship we had with the Father was everything.

As a teacher, one of the things I learned was that if I loved a subject I taught very often I imparted my love for it to my students. The reverse was also true. At one point in teaching, I was asked to teach world history. Well, I really do not enjoy history and had a hard time coming up with a way to make the class exciting. I can ensure you that none of my former students ever became history scholars. You see, my students became excited about what I was excited about and well....

I raise this point because I believe you cannot instill a passion in your children for something you are not passionate about yourself. I have witnessed couples who grew up in church and believed their children should as well send their kids on Sunday morning to the local Chuch but not attend services themselves. I have also watched these same children stop going to church the minute mom and dad stopped making them. In this particular case, mom and dad don't really see church as a lifesaving, vital thing for their own lives, and children realize that if it is not important to mom and dad, then it really doesn't need to be important to them either.

I have also seen parents who were of separate denominations before marriage who never really talked through the issue before children. Here the children seem to get stuck in the middle of a battle they cannot even begin to understand. They are still at the tender stage of trying to understand if there is a God and what that means; they definitely cannot understand that there is a God but He somehow makes mommy and daddy fight about the best way to worship Him and which building to take them to. Sometimes I fear as adults we have lost sight of what is really important when it comes to the things we expose our children too.

Then, of course, you have the whole issue of the believer who is married to an unbeliever and the complete confusion this can cause a child. When God spoke to the Israelites about raising their children up to understand they were His chosen people, He was very specific that it was to be an everyday, all the time, in every situation thing for them. God means business when it comes to the souls of the children He places in our care. Therefore, if you are in any of the situations I have described, I challenge you and your spouse to have a heart-to-heart discussion about the importance of God in your lives. Iron out the issues that can cause your sweet children to stumble, and get serious about your mandate to raise a child of the Most High God.

Then I challenge you to take a serious look at your own relationship with the Father. You cannot teach something you do not know, and you cannot impart something that is not in your heart. Make sure God is number one in your own life so that you will have what you need to bring that lifesaving, amazing relationship to your children too. There really is nothing you can do that will give you all the tools you need to raise your children than spending time with God in worship, prayer and in the study of His Word. Then let His life flow from you to them.

JERRY

Thinking of God as my Father, and as The Father, has been one of the most impactive revelations of my life. As a youngster, I learned about the Almighty God and that doing bad things made Him mad and hell was a real place. I tried not to anger this all-powerful deity and stayed away as far as I could without making Him think I was avoiding Him. I knew Jesus was His Son and that He gave His life for me, but I never saw how I could live up to the expectations to be as good as He was. Those juvenile impressions did not resolve as I got older; they became more intense. God was bigger and more powerful than I had realized, and Jesus's standard of perfection was absolutely unachievable. My fear of God was at the peak of the meter and my understanding of His love for me was barely moving the needle.

After Debbie and I met, she loaned me a book by Floyd McClung titled *The Father Heart of God,* and my world shifted from fearing a distant, stuffy rule maker to accepting the love of a gracious parent. Reading through the Bible with this new filter, I was amazed at all the

JERRY AND DEBBIE BURBEE

examples of our Father loving His children, involving provision, identity, character, correction, mercy, and grace. The shift was easy for me because my dad was involved in my life in caring, constructive ways, but, as the book pointed out, the image of our earthly father very much influences our perception of God as Father. Just as I played catch with my dad, I now could have that time with Father God. Over the years, Father and I have sang together, hashed out confusing concepts, corrected inappropriate behaviors, and walked and talked about what was worrying me. The relationship Jesus had with the Father is the type of relationship I can have with God. John 14-17 blew my mind with all its descriptions of Jesus and His Father, how I/we are included, and that He even gives us His very Spirit to comfort and guide us. I still have some of my father's "dad-isms", which occasionally pop up when certain situations arise ("If you are going to do a job, do it right or don't do it at all." "Anything can be fixed with duct tape, an old milk jug, and a strand of bailing wire.") Now, I recognize that the Holy Spirit inside me, and the effort I applied to knowing Scripture, was Father God "dad-isms" to the millionth extreme. The nearly adversarial relationship I had had with Him was beginning to melt.

Parents make mistakes, and those mistakes have consequences. It was not until I was standing at my dad's coffin that I realized the depth of his love for me, even though in my mind I never thought I was good enough for him. His manner of encouragement and my manner of receiving that encouragement never meshed well, leaving me with the impression that he only noticed my failures. In that tearful moment of clarity, I also realized I viewed Father God the same way. That insight is what Floyd McClung was trying to describe and it is essential to maturing in a relationship with Father God. Our dads, as good or as bad as they are or have been, set the initial expectations of how we expect Father God to interact with us, and every earthly father misses the mark somewhere along the way. When I discovered this gem, I was able to make peace with my dad's strengths and weaknesses and not hold Father God to the same expectations I changed how I prayed and read the Bible as the way to get to know Him as He wants to be known.

The next big step came when I realized that Father God looked at me like I look at my children, only even better. To think that my kids were scared of me, or assumed I was always going to be mad at them, broke my heart. I was nearly devastated when I discovered that is actually what they felt at times. My heart broke for Father God because for if my kids acting that way affected me as it did, I can't imagine how crushed He must have felt when I reject His mercy, thought He didn't care about me, or how I was an inconvenience He merely tolerated. Allowing myself to expect this intimacy from the Father and allowing myself to experience it are the new foundation of the father I try to be. Having a healthy relationship with Father God is not merely another mandatory task necessary to avoid destruction, it is the heart of being a parent. How you see Him as Father is how you will parent your children.

Regardless of the relationship you have had with your earthly father(s), regardless of your past and current relationship with Father God, and regardless of how you have parented up to this point, what Jesus described in John chapters 14-17 is what is available for us to enjoy. Through Jesus, we are loved by the Father and can dwell forever in His love. That's how He feels about us and that's how we feel about our children.

CHAPTER 16
MARRIAGE COMES FIRST

DEBBIE

I have a plaque in my room that reads "I was not made to be subtle." I can assure you no one in my family would disagree with that plaque, and I understand I have laid it on pretty heavily about the sacrifice it takes to parent a child. In truth, God did not ask you to do it alone. I know some single parents will read this book, so I want to preface that I am speaking to God's ideal, involving a man and a woman getting married and raising a family together. I also know there might be a million reasons why you might not be doing things the ideal way. So my encouragement to you is that God says He will be our husband or bride. When I talk about how to support each other emotionally, you will have to go to God for everything and that's not bad; He is our ultimate source. When I talk about practical physical ways to support each other, I want you to know the Bible says in Mark 10:29-30 that God will give us homes, brothers, sisters, mothers, children, and fields a hundred times in this present age. That for you is the church. My encouragement to you is do not be too prideful to reach out to your church family for support and help. Let them have the joy of being in your child's life.

Jerry and I did not live near our biological families due to God's plan for our lives. However, we have an amazing church family, and I thank

God for the other mothers and fathers, grandparents, brothers and sisters, and aunts and uncles He gave my kids. Beautiful people like the Smoyers and the Hutchens who were stand-in grandparents for them. Families, like the Huffs and so many more, who came to games and productions just to watch my children because they loved them like aunts and uncles. So, believe me, I am sure there are people in your church who would be honored to take those places in your child's life. Just swallow your pride and ask. Then watch the faithfulness of God and His people amaze you.

To those of us who are married, I say praise God He didn't plan this parenting thing to be done all alone. Face it, having someone depend on you 100 percent, 24/7 can be exhausting. Thus, God planned for children to have a mother and a father. Having a strong marriage is essential to having a healthy family. Do not neglect your marriage! I understand you are busy raising your family, we all are, but your marriage has to come first. When our children were younger, Jerry and I did a fair job with this, but I must confess we got too secure in our marriage when our kids were older. We believed our marriage closeness would be fine even though we had been warned to be sure to spend time on just the two of us. We were so happy as a family and did so much together that we as a couple thought that made our relationship fine. It wasn't until our children did the very thing we had trained them for and left the nest that we realized we were in trouble. We were not as close as we had thought.

Now, if you are like a lot of couples, us included, you maybe had two years together before you had your first child. You found your dream mate, the one you had been praying for, and you could not stand to be apart. You couldn't hardly wait for the wedding day so you didn't have to say goodbye and go your separate ways. You had fun as a couple; you were really getting to know each other. Then came the first baby. From that point on, you had to fight hard to maintain the connection of a couple, that unit we lovingly call the "us", because the needs of the family came first.

When our children left home, I remember crying a lot, but I also remember looking at Jerry and thinking that at one point in our lives we felt really full as a couple. We wanted children, but we were very content together. We never lacked for things to do together and always had lots to talk about. In fact, I really loved that about him, our conversations. But now, I looked at him and wondered what we would talk about without the kids being the center of our conversations. In fact, statistically it is scary how many marriages fall apart at this point, between twenty-five and thirty years of marriage. We all have heard the excuse "We drifted apart." You are constantly growing and changing as a person, and so is your mate.

Maintaining a strong marriage comes with two major benefits. One, it keeps your children healthy and happy. Two, it ensures you can run the rest of your race strong. You see, most of us will return to the original plan of "you and me against the world" after the children leave. We may still have thirty or more years left together. We still need to pursue the plan God has for us as a couple. I will say that since Jerry and I became empty nesters it feels like God has brought us bigger and sometimes crazier challenges which have grown a bigger faith in us than I could've ever imagined. All of this will be hard to accomplish if you haven't taken care of your marriage. Jerry and I had some ground to make up because we had put our marriage on hold. Please, learn from us and fight to keep your marriage strong while raising your family.

I know all the excuses you are making for why you don't do this. Believe me, I probably used every one of them. When it comes down to it, usually our priorities are wrong. Trust me when I say your kids will be fine if you go away for a weekend to pour into your marriage and seek God together. Now, I won't say you won't face trials when you do this. One time when our son, Michael, was two, we went to St. Louis for a weekend. I don't remember exactly why (think we stopped at an arcade to play on our way) but it took longer than planned to get there. We didn't have cell phones yet, so when we got to our hotel we had several messages waiting to call our sitter, the daycare, and the hospital. I went into panic mode. We came to find out Michael had fallen and hit his head on a rolling chalkboard. He needed stitches. I felt sick inside and was internally vowing never to go away again. But God had taken care of Michael in every way. At the daycare, he was very spoiled by one of our closest friends, David , Michael went everywhere with David; Michael even called him "my David." Well, it was David who took him to the hospital. Jerry worked in the ER, and the nurse who took care of Michael was one we lovingly called "Grandma Di." We had forgotten to leave a permission note this trip, but the ER staff knew David was a trusted part of our family. They took his consent to treat. To this day, Michael remembers why he has the scar on his head, but were it not for us telling the story, he would not remember much about the experience and our absence from it. I know 100 percent that I was way more traumatized than Michael, but that was due to my lack of faith in God to cover my kids.

So down goes excuse number one. That your children need you to be with them or they will not be ok if you go away. The rest, like lack of time or resources etc... can fall just as easy. Prioritize your time with your spouse. Save up for going away together, meaning budget for it. If the reality is that you really can't afford a trip away, be creative. We have couples who come use our finished basement as a getaway. They come and hide out from the world to spend time with each other and God. I'm sure you can find similar places in your church community. Think out of the box. Send your kids somewhere and use your own house as your getaway. Whatever you do, the important thing is that you do it.

Your kids need you to be a united front. There is nothing more powerful to show the faithfulness of God than parents who love each other. The divorce rate in the Church should not be the same as in the world. People say divorce does not affect children, but usually those words come from selfish people who want to justify their own sin or selfishness. I'm not saying there are not legitimate reasons for divorce, but so often even those in the Church justify something that God does not. My parents are in their eighties and my world would still be rocked if they chose to divorce. Their marriage has always brought security to my life. Yes, children survive a divorce, but do you want children who are simply trying to survive? Don't you want healthy, thriving children? The best thing I ever did for my children was love their father biblically.

I could write forever on having a strong marriage. In fact, the world is full of marriage books. If you are someone who is really serious about your walk with God, I recommend *You and Me Forever* by Francis and Lisa Chan. It is actually free on the website www.youandmeforever.org. There are a lot of good resources out there, so ask around. I'm sure your church leadership has marriage books they recommend.

The point I want to make here is that your children may be your number one disciples, but the Bible says you and your spouse are to be one. You are not supposed to do this alone. Make sure you keep your marriage relationship on fire and your union strong.

Now, I would like to take a moment to speak to husbands. I believe there has been a fallacy in the thinking of most men that is a holdover from the 1950s. That fallacy is that kids are the woman's responsibility. I am sure a lot of you are saying, "Oh no, I don't think that way. I help with the kids." Really? You just proved my point. What do you mean "you help with them"? Aren't they your kids too? Let's face it father, when was the last time you stopped before making plans and said, "Wait, I need to make sure my wife is okay to watch the kids." I can guarantee she cannot just assume you will cover them so she can go out with the girls.

Gentleman, let's come into this century. It is almost impossible in this day and age to have a one income household, s it is very likely your wife works full time too. Gone are the days where the little wifey stays home to take care of the house and children. Too many men are still functioning as if their job is merely to bring home the bacon and her job is the house and kids. The problem is she spends forty hours bringing home the bacon too. Not to mention, it is your house, and they are your kids as well. Did you hear me? They are your kids too! Get off your duff and share the responsibilities.

I can remember times when my husband wanted a romantic night out, so he would say, "Hey, let's have a date night Friday." By the time I had planned the date, found a babysitter, got the kids fed, and made sure

JERRY AND DEBBIE BURBEE

everything else was taken care of all I wanted to do was crash. I was exhausted, and he couldn't understand why I wasn't gazing into his eyes lovingly. Romance is hard when you are dead on your feet. I hope you got my point, gentlemen.

Step up, men, and become responsible for your homes. You will be surprised how sexy a man is who cleans up the dishes and puts the kids to bed so his wife can have a moment to rest or better yet spend time with God.

Once again, our focus in this book is parenting and a strong marriage is so important for good parenting. I want to add that to have a strong marriage you must remember God is the only one who can fill you with purpose and make you more like Christ. You cannot get that from your spouse. Don't expect them to be the fourth person of the Godhead. A side note for women here. Sometimes we expect our husband to be omniscient and know what we need or desire. When we do that, we set them up to fail. Only God is omniscient. If you desire something from your husband don't expect him to just know it, tell him. When you come together with your spouse, be sure to come full of God. Be sure you are bringing strength to the us, making it full of God's purpose. It is okay to need strength from your spouse at times. We all have weak moments, but we cannot expect our spouse to be our only source of getting our needs met. That must be God.

I could continue speaking on marriage but the last thing I want to mention is not talk to your children in a negative way about your spouse ever. Children have no clue how to deal with it when we talk harshly about their daddy or mommy to them, especially teenagers. I don't care how mature your teenager might seem, they cannot help with your marriage. Parents talk to each other about the kids but never talk to the kids about you mate. No excuses here. I don't care how justified you might feel about whatever you want to complain about concerning your spouse. **Do not do it.** Go talk to God about your spouse, but I must warn you He may talk to you about your own shortcomings when you do.

Life just gets hard sometimes. When Jerry was in medical school and residency, he had to work long hours. Sometimes in residency it was normal for him to work eighty to one hundred hours a week. I never complained to my children about this. In fact, I included Daddy in everything when I talked to them. I also made a big deal about the when he was home with us. When he walked in the door, everything stopped and we yelled, "Daddy's home!" All three children raced to his side screaming with joy. I can tell you that time in our life was really challenging, but if you ask my children, they do not remember things that way at all. They remember Daddy being there a lot. The way you talk about your spouse to your children is very important.

Moms, I will also add that the way you talk about your spouse to others when you think your children are not listening is just as important. Believe me, they are always listening. Control your tongue, and if you have an issue with your spouse, once again I say take it to God in prayer. Don't be surprised should you learn you may be the one who needs to repent. In Psalms 45, God talks about the woman who honors her husband. He says she will have sons who become kings.

JERRY

One of the objectives of parenting is to train our children so they have healthy relationships with the people in their lives. As mentioned earlier, love and honor are the foundation of healthy relationships. What we demonstrate in the relationship we have with our spouse is one that will set our children's standards of normal. Do your words and actions harmonize with love and honor or is disrespect the off-key screech that sets your family on edge? Your children will hear that marriage is one of the most important relationships a person can have. They will see all sorts of craziness from Hollywood. The stories and experiences with friends and extended family also will give them a broad view of what can happen in marriage. You will have ample opportunity to explain: "Aunt Gilda and Uncle Fredrick are mean to each other, but that's not the way God wants us to behave." You will choose your words carefully about why their friend's parents are getting a divorce. But how you and your spouse treat one another is the most impactful. What are you demonstrating?

My poor wife has had to tolerate thirty years of my intestinal issues. As ignorant male teens, my friends and I would gladly share the fruit of last night's chili, gagging and holding our noses while we laughed. Debbie, however, has no appreciation for the odiferous expressions of teenage boys. On a long ride in the car on a cold day with the windows rolled up tightly, I would proudly share what I had been storing up inside of me. Instead of laughter and a return-in-kind, she would quickly roll down the window while gagging and look at me with the WIFE stare. Being the slow clod that I am, I kept trying to impress her, but, the reaction was always the same. I wouldn't openly do this around other people, only people I loved and those whom I knew loved me. I was sharing the deepest parts of my inner self; I was being vulnerable. Yet Debbie did not ever appreciate it. Finally (and I believe it was during her first pregnancy when nausea was intense), she stirred the courage to tell me (actually I think she phrased it as "Do that again and I will puke on you"). Flabbergasted, I felt rejected, accosted, minimalized, restrained, and disappointed all rolled into one. After refusing to accept that something so precious to me was offensive to her, I pushed the boundaries. She politely swallowed her vomit, but would remind me that it was displeasing to her. Even if I made a game out of it, she wouldn't join in. No jokes softened the blow. I am embarrassed to say that she finally had to come out and say it (these aren't her exact words, but they recreate the meaning): "Jerry, when you do that I feel like you don't respect me. I have asked you nicely. I have threatened you. I have tried to ignore it. But it seems to me that flatulence is more important to you than I am." You have reached a new low when you value the stench of dung over your wife.

But, we all know, it's not about the gas, it's about respect. In your marriage, are you showing effuse love and honor or are you passing gas?

Looking back over the years, there are hundreds of moments I would like to do over. How I responded when she asked for help when I was in the middle of doing something that was obviously more important. The clueless assumption that I could go play basketball while she watched the kids without even asking her if she had the time. The countless other assumptions, such as taking for granted that all those things that needed to be done that I did not want to do she would take care of. The dirty dishes in the sink were as much mine as they were hers. She was not the only one who knew how to operate the vacuum cleaner. I did not value her. I even got close to assuming I deserved her service. This pattern of behavior is one way the sins of the parents are passed to the children. They saw it all. I was setting my children's expectations for relationships.

Fortunately, God's mercy and grace arrested me early. I came into our marriage with some baggage. My pride and arrogance did not like laying down my life for my wife like Jesus did for the Church. However, I had to decide what atmosphere I wanted in my home. Love and honor do not grow in a house where the parents disrespect each other and the children are not held accountable to do the same. It also does not grow when the parents say one thing then do another.

Do you protect your spouse's vulnerabilities? Are you guilty of using them for your amusement or advantage whenever possible? When your spouse attempts to engage, where are you? Do you lash out when confronted? Are you always defending yourself? Do you take time to look deeply into each other's eyes for that spark that started this journey? Are you so offended by what has happened that you have closed off your heart? You may not even be aware where disrespect has poisoned you. Alternately, you may be aware but are afraid to confess or confront it. Can you listen? Can you be humble? If not, you may need help. Take the time to get it. If you are like I was and are having trouble honoring your spouse, you probably have some deep, personal issues that need to be dealt with. It will not happen overnight, but I know from experience that the Lord will help you if you ask for it.

Being a little thick headed, I needed some very direct help. I asked Debbie what made her feel cherished and honored. At first, she was uneasy about revealing these special areas. I was asking her to be vulnerable and I had not proved being the most trustworthy in handling sensitive issues. If I treated them jokingly or disregarded them like I had with other issues, I was setting her up for deep injury.

Unfortunately, I now know this from experience. But Debbie took a chance and began with easy things. She told me she really liked it when I opened the door for her. A simple thing that I had to make a conscious effort to do started the process of me not thinking of myself and transformed me into a husband who sought to show honor and love to his wife. I noticed one day that she was having difficulty carrying our clothes hampers down the stairs to do the laundry. I asked if I could start doing the laundry. It took patience on her part as she had to teach me not to put the red stuff in with the white stuff and other such details. I had to humble myself to allow her to teach me the way she wanted it done and the timing of when to get it done. Yet I learned her way, and if I thought I had a better idea, I ran it by her first to make sure there were no flaws in my plans. As I became more focused on honoring her, I began to notice some of the things I said jokingly were painful to her. In time, Debbie began to develop enough trust in me to point some of these out, and I was open to hearing them. Again, this did not happen overnight, and many, many mistakes were made, but I began to notice that the way I treated my wife impacted the way my children treated her as their mother.

Another hurdle I had to clear was the expectation of her praise. I thought showing love and honor would result in effusive praise for how wonderful I was. I thought she would be amazed at how self-sacrificing I was being. Warning: If you are doing something so that you will be praised for it, that's not love or honor. Love, honor, and respect are given because the person receiving your action deserves it. They are the focus of the praise, not you. If the receiving person does not acknowledge your action, that has no bearing on whether they were worthy of the action. God loved us even when we did not love him. If the receiver shares in the gift, it is a great moment for both parties. Seek to live in a place where your joy comes from honoring her, not in receiving praise for your actions. Become so enthralled with your spouse that your words and acts of love have to be expressed or you will explode. Do this not to please her, not to try to earn something, not to look good but because loving and honoring her is the nature of who you are.

As I grew in awareness, I began to notice and appreciate things Debbie had been doing for me. Every day when I came home from the hospital, as soon as I stepped in the door, I heard Debbie yell, "DADDY'S HOME!" Soon she and all the kids would come running and tackle me. I was covered with hugs and kisses and showered with the excitement of their day. No matter how my day had been, I was adored and honored at home. I initially thought my wonderfulness had spontaneously generated this response. I have since found out that Debbie purposely trained our children to act this way. This was not a forced behavior. It was the honor she had for me being transferred into them. Even though I would be gone for long hours and wasn't around on weekends, she wanted them, and me, to enjoy it when I was home. It would have been easy for her to complain about me not being around, but instead her honor for me won out. And now for me, those are some of the most pleasant memories of my life.

If your marriage is full of love and honor, the openings for disrespect are minimal. If your children live under a marriage that displays respect, it will be easier for them to live that way as well. Some of our children's deepest scars are the result of the disrespect Debbie and I showed to each other. However, I also think some of our children's depth and stability arose from the love and honor we lived.

Some of our recommendations for a strong marriage:

1. Go away at least once a year for a long weekend to spend time seeking God about direction for your marriage, children, and life together.
2. Be very intentional about reserving a time together to pray.
3. Have a family devotional time.
4. At least once a year, go away and do something fun for just the two of you.
5. Spend your date night focusing your conversation on each other and what God is doing, not just on your children.
6. Give each other a chance to talk without interruptions.
7. Listen.

8. Try to understand what the other is saying as well as why they are saying it.
9. Ask questions for clarity, not to lead to a solution or to prove a point.
10. Only offer solutions or opinions when requested.
11. Be humble enough to give and receive feedback on how well you listen.
12. Keep track of each other's dreams and learn how to encourage each other in seeing them fulfilled.
13. Set aside time every day to verbalize what you appreciate about each other by making two statements that begin with "What I appreciate about you is...."
14. Have ground rules for fighting. Here are some of ours:
15. The possibility of divorce is never mentioned.
16. This establishes that escape is not an option.
17. This creates the expectation that the problem will be resolved.
18. Pulling out the "big guns" is always off limits.
19. Examples:
20. "You don't love me or you would ...."
21. "You're just like your mother (or some other unsavory person)."
22. Avoid using terms of absolute"
23. "You ALWAYS..."
24. "You NEVER..."
25. Remember, the enemy is not your spouse but the accuser who is trying to destroy your marriage.
26. When a fight has developed:
27. Take time to pause and remind yourself and your spouse that you love each other and act accordingly.
28. Focus on the issue and not on the symptoms.
29. Avoid being baited by the enemy to pull up past wounds.
30. Remember that repentance means the sins are cast away and not to be revived as ammunition.
31. For most men, we need to realize our wife's strong emotions are an expression of her need for closeness, not an attack.

32. For most women, we need to realize your husband's silence may be a defense against accusations or badgering.
33. Find creative ways to be romantic.
34. Leave a note for your spouse.
35. Bring home a simple gift that demonstrates you are thinking about your spouse.
36. Text sweet expressions and emotions during the day.
37. Brush your teeth before getting close.
38. Slow dance by candle light after putting the kids to bed.
39. Enjoy romance for romance sake, not only as foreplay.
40. Guard against taking your spouse for granted.
41. Everyone desires to be noticed and appreciated.
42. Everyone wants to be seen.
43. God continually woos us into deeper fellowship. Enjoy constantly wooing your spouse into a more intimate relationship.
44. The magic in the relationship does not have to weaken or die, but it does take intentional effort to keep the fire burning.
45. Always guard against situations that might put you in potentially compromising circumstances.
46. Always avoid privately discussing intimate issues with a member of the opposite sex. If that person needs counsel for his/her issues, seek to connect the individual with your spouse instead.
47. The enemy looks for subtle ways to drag us into inappropriate relationships.
48. When you said "I do" you acknowledged that God was joining you in marriage. Always remember God will not change His mind about your joining that day.
49. Look for ways that others can pour into your children and give you a chance to get away alone.
50. Our friends, Wendell and Kathy, have a cousins' camp every summer.
51. They get a week to connect with their grandchildren.
52. The cousins who do not live near each other get a chance to be together.

53. Mom and dad get a week by themselves.
54. Alternate Friday night babysitting with other couples.

If you want to raise children who are emotionally healthy and respectful, begin by letting love and honor consume your every thought and action, especially towards your spouse.

SECTION THREE

Our final section is about the mandate God has given us to train our children. In fact it is a mandate that contains a promise, being that if we train them in God's ways that when they are old they will not depart from it. The goal we had for our children was that they grow up loving God so deeply that they would never depart from that. The following chapters are ones we hope will bring light to this topic.

CHAPTER 17
MANDATE TO TRAIN

DEBBIE

Proverbs 22:6 says to train up a child in the way he should go and when he is old he will not depart from it. Almost every young Christian parent knows this verse; in fact it is one most of us can quote word for word. Jerry and I were no exception. From the start of our marriage, we began to pray that God would give us a godly legacy, one that would still be found faithfully serving Jesus on the day of His return. When we had our first child, I began to pray about this Proverbs verse with more diligence. During one of those prayer sessions, God spoke to me about this verse in a way that totally revolutionized the way I thought about it.

The best way I can summarize what God began to show me is to use the illustration of training my child to brush her teeth. When I began to train her to brush her teeth I did not simply place tooth paste and a toothbrush in her little hands and say, "Here my child, this is the way to have clean teeth and a cavity free life." No, first I brushed her teeth for her before she was even able to understand what teeth were, or have any. Then as she grew, I began to show her how I was brushing my teeth. Next, I let her brush hers by herself, checking her work and frequently (at first) redoing the job. Then she graduated to me telling her every morning and night to be sure to brush her teeth. When the first cavity came along, we kind of started the whole process all over. Eventually, there came a day when my child no longer had to be told to brush her teeth because she enjoyed having clean teeth and no cavities herself. That is how you train, through patient instruction and modeling.

Parenting is not for the faint of heart. We can never grow weary or lazy in training because God said it is **our** responsibility to train our little ones in the ways of God and life. Training does not stop until your child leaves the nest. God said that if I wanted a godly legacy, then I must train my child in His ways. Just as diligently as I trained my daughter to brush her teeth, I had to train her to read her Bible and to worship and seek God for herself. It was my mandate to teach her the prayer of petition and the prayer of intercession. I was ordered to teach, no, train her, how deep cries out to deep in the prayer closet. It was also my task to be sure she understood what it means to pray without ceasing. You see, if I had just taken my child to church or sent her alone, then I would not be training her in anything and the Proverbs 22 promise would not belong to me.

The other thing I knew deep in my heart was that it would not matter how many wonderful works I did for God in the end if my children did not make it to heaven. She and her brothers have been given to me as my number one disciples, and if I walked into eternity without them, then in my own eyes I will have failed.

JERRY

The idea of training brings two images to mind. First, it's hard to train someone to do something you do not know how to do yourself. We knew it would be good for the kids to learn how to play the piano, but neither of us could play. I wanted to teach them how to fish, but I wasn't very good at it, so we never went. I did know how to play basketball and some of my fondest memories are throwing elbows with my sons, trying to get position under the basket, then hearing the stories of their games when they laid it on like Pops taught them. I knew if I wanted to train my kids to follow hard after God, it wasn't going to happen if I didn't know how or if I excused myself because I was not very good at it to the point of not trying. I spent years being trained in basketball skills and then practiced. I learned to look for the open man and when to pass or take the shot. Through my sweat, I taught my boys how to sweat.

Likewise, through my hours of Bible study, seasons of repentance, glorious experiences in His presence, iron-sharpening-iron moments, and wave upon wave of His goodness, mercy, and grace, I have learned how to box out the devil, how to set a screen so another player can score, how to drive to the goal with no fear of being stopped, and how to recover from a missed shot. These things I taught my children. The joy of the game and the glory of the sweat are not understood by those on the sidelines, but the folks banging under the basket, sprinting to the other end to get open or to play defense wouldn't have it any other way. Debbie would not have bothered to teach our kids how to brush her teeth if she didn't know how to do it or didn't like to do it.

Others can certainly help, as we had piano teachers for the kids, and Grandpa taught them how to fish for salmon, but even those teaching moments were dependent upon us being involved. Debbie took them to piano lessons and made sure they practiced. She and I both went along so the kids could fish with Grandpa. There might be specific skills not in your possession, but you do have a relationship with God. You have experiences, you have knowledge, and you have the opportunity to learn more so you can train more. The likelihood that your children will have healthy teeth diminishes greatly if you don't take care of your teeth and teach them to do the same. More than likely, your kids will follow God just like you train and model for them.

Second, the idea of training recalls to mind the very unpleasant memory of the first week of basketball practice and running wind sprints until half the team is dry heaving over the trash can. As a player, I thought it was the cruelest thing that could be done to someone who just wants to play the game. "Let's play. Why do we got to do all this conditioning?" Years later, when I had the opportunity to help coach my sons' basketball teams, my perspective changed 180 degrees. I began to recall games where my team lost because we ran out of stamina in the fourth quarter. I used to play one-on-one with a friend who was a much better player than I, but I could keep the game close because he got tired quicker than I did. Standing as the coach, with the responsibility of preparing a team for competition, I knew the boring drills and stupid wind sprints could be the difference between winning and losing. It was difficult listening to the groans of the beasts pleading for the torture to stop, and to know when enough was enough or if I had gone too far.

How to make training enjoyable, or at least have it understood as a necessary part of the process, is the mark of a good trainer and a good trainee. Presenting a vision of what the training is leading to, aiding successful completion of short-term and long-term goals, and taking ownership of the process are three of the fundamentals. If you can show your child positive examples of faithful disciples, it helps them look past the present difficulties. Debbie and I would tell stories about people we knew, have people in our home who lived what we were aiming for, and read books to the kids about men and women of faith. (One of my favorites was *Brucho.*) We would have discussions about our family Bible reading, their own Bible reading, or something mentioned at church. I loved to hear their perspectives, even at four or five years of age, because we gave them a platform to express thoughts about they had processed themselves, gently correcting if needed, but mostly showing they were successful in gaining understanding. We also stressed their relationship with God was what they made it. We helped and guided, but we could not make them live Jesus; that was theirs to find and develop. It can be easy to confuse training and performance. Sometimes poor outcomes are the result of poor training. Sometimes poor outcomes spring from a lack of desire and effort by the trainee. When I took possession of my relationship with God as a young man, my parents' encouragement was no longer forced behaviors; instead they echoed my internal decision. That type of ownership is what we fostered in our kids. I can help but the sooner they take ownership the better.

Training requires commitment and patience. Getting in shape doesn't occur in a couple of days; it is a lifestyle. Training promotes changes that develop a lifestyle necessary for the contest. The contest we and our children face is a war against the powers and principalities of evil in which poor training, poor effort, and lack of ownership can result in disaster.

CHAPTER 18
MORE IS CAUGHT THAN TAUGHT

DEBBIE

There are some topics in parenting that seem obvious because they have been an accepted concept for awhile, so I don't want to insult anyone by writing a whole chapter that would be discourteous. However, I do not want to neglect something as important as the idea that our children will be shaped by our lives and our actions far more than they will by our words. There is that rare moment when my child quotes my own words back to me, but far more often they have learned more from my heart by watching the way I live day in and day out because that seems to be so much louder. I can also say that nothing frustrates a child more than a parent that says one thing but lives something else. The old adage "Do as I say, not as I do" never really works.

Very frequently parents make a horrible mistake of thinking their children are not paying attention. Well, they are always paying attention! If you don't believe me, just watch your young child and notice how many things they do that mirror you or your spouse. When Michael was in daycare, I noticed he always had his sweatpants pulled up above his calves. I remember thinking how funny it was, wondering why he did it. Then on a Saturday, as I was cleaning the house, I realized that because I was mopping the floors and cleaning the bathtub, I had pulled my sweatpants above my calves. Oh my, mystery solved.

Children do listen to what you say, but more importantly they watch every move their parents make. When mom and dad preach that lying is a sin, and maybe even brings out scripture after scripture in an attempt to get Johnny to stop lying, but think the little white lies they tell don't matter, well, let me just say they are sorely mistaken. In fact, when Jerry and I found that if we were dealing with an issue in one of our children and we couldn't find a breakthrough, almost always when we sought God about it, we found that until that thing was completely dealt with in one of us we would never find a solution. If you find yourself banging your head against the wall when dealing with something in your child, we would tell you to go pray, and to be ready because you might not be so happy with what God reveals in you.

I started this chapter talking about the inconsistency of sin in our lives, but this variance can also be true for areas where we speak a good passion game yet our follow-through when no one is watching flounders. For example, when life throws you a curveball, do you worry and fret or do you get on our knees and pray? When you are hanging out at home, what plays on your radio? Do your kids hear you grumble about things or would they describe you as a thankful person? What about your brothers and sisters in Christ, how do you talk about them? How do you talk about your spouse? Yep, it all matters and nothing gets by your children's observation.

If you want children who are passionate worshippers, they need to learn that from you. If you want them to believe God when they pray, they must see that kind of faith in you. When somebody does something for you, do you show gratitude? Do you tell your children the stories of God's time-tested faithfulness? If your children haven't heard your salvation story, then you better get to talking! Tell them how God brought you together with your spouse. Proclaim His goodness and faithfulness over and over. Sometimes we talk more to our kids about our favorite movies than we do about what Jesus and our salvation mean to us.

In Deuteronomy 11:18-21, God talks about how we are to teach our children the words of God. He says to talk about them when we sit at home and when we walk along the road, when we lie down and when we get up. From the commentaries I've read, the children of Israel took this scripture to heart, and at every occasion, they would read or discuss the Torah in their gathering. They frequently quoted Scripture and retold the stories of Moses, David, and Abraham. The same should be true concerning our stories when it comes to the awesomeness of our God. I have been a Christian for over fifty years, and I can tell you from many years of walking with God that if I pay attention, not one day of my life goes by without God's mercy and love surrounding me and intervening on my behalf.

I could go into a lot of details in this chapter to try to cover this topic, but I think the thing I would like to challenge you with is to go before God and ask the Holy Spirit to show you where in your life you have duality. Duality is where you hold two opposing views on a topic and they can't both coexist as truth. Yesterday, we were talking with some friends about the series "The Chosen." It is a retelling of Jesus's life on Earth and they have taken the liberty of filling in some of the blanks in the everyday life of Jesus and the disciples. Some people like it; some do not. I'm not here to debate that part. In the first episode of season one, the series focuses on Mary Magdalene, whom we know lived a life of sin and was demonized before she encountered Jesus. The Bible tells us Jesus delivered her of many demons. Our friends said the show scared their young son, and one of his comments about it was that he did not realize demons were real. Now, this is a simple childlike duality but exemplifies how something in the Bible can be a good story, but not the reality we live in. My husband talks about what it was like the day he was sitting in his high school AP biology class and suddenly realized that the caveman stories and the Biblical story of Adam and Eve were in opposition to each other. He had compartmentalized the two stories to two different realities, school and church, and was blown away that such a separation was not viable or healthy, but it was how he had managed the discrepancies. He never let the two worlds overlap.

Sometimes we can be so entrenched in our duality that we do not realize a part of our life, or the way we are living, is not the way God has said for His people to live. Duality can say that you believe something to be true, but our lives tell a different story. You see, if I truly believe something, then my life will prove that out. For example, I could say all day long that I am a Republican, but if I vote for every Democrat when I get to the voting booth, then the truth is I am really a Democrat. Now, I know this example is a little out there, but I hope it gets my point across with a little humor. We live out what we truly believe.

Usually our duality will show up in more subtle ways, like a woman who says she believes it is God's will for her to honor her husband, but when she is together with her friends, she does not hesitate to join the crowd in voicing her frustrations about her husband. Does this describe anyone you know? Yourself? Maybe we are able to hold our tongues but we just nod in agreement with everything they say. If you are like me, you will find when God reveals your duality, it will be shocking to you, and you will be truly surprised to find where it has been hiding. Even scarier is when God uses one of your older children to point out a place where you are doing something different from the way you used to do, or the way you taught them to do it.

You see, our very observant children see our duality more clearly than we do at times. They become very confused when our words do not match our actions. "Be careful little eyes what you see" is a line from an old children's song, but for us parents, I think the line should declare, "Be careful because little eyes will see."

JERRY

I used to assume everything I said would be understood and valued by others with the same veracity I had as I treasured these pearls of wisdom. When the reality of this faulty assumption struck me, I realized managing my assumptions about others should be high on my priority list. Assuming that a piece of knowledge has been incorporated into another person's psyche can lead to mayhem, which

I am sure all of us have encountered. In parenting, I found that assuming my kids understood my instructions, my passions, or my logic led to chaos, frustration, and calamity. Even worse is assuming that something that flirts with unrighteousness will not influence my child, even though it does not bother me. When we watched movies with our kids, frequently we stopped to identify and discuss elements that were contrary to our lifestyle so they understood these discrepancies. I recognized what may be miniscule in me has the potential of becoming enormous in my kids. I think Jehoshaphat was guilty of such an assumption in how he included his son, Jehoram, in his dealings with Ahab.

First Kings 12 records the prophesied separation of Judah and Israel, as Rehoboam and Jeroboam become the kings of these now separate kingdoms. As we move through the rest of the book, we see the two kingdoms were almost always at war with each other until 1 Kings 22:44 reveals that Jehoshaphat made peace with the king of Israel. First Kings gives the account of all the evil Ahab and his father, Omri, released in Israel. In 2 Chronicles 14-17. we read about all the good things Asa and Jehoshaphat do in Judah. In 2 Chronicles 18, we see how Jehoshaphat acquired peace with Israel: He made a marriage alliance with Ahab by uniting his son, Jehoram, the next king of Judah, with Ahab's daughter. The next few chapters tell of the good things that Jehoshaphat did, and 2 Kings 3:14 shows the respect Elisha had for him. I expect that Jehoshaphat sought to extend the Godly legacy to his sons by teaching them the ways of the Lord, or at least had them taught by the priests and other knowledgeable men. Yet, when we look at Jehoram's life, he was more drawn to the ways of Ahab than the ways of Jehoshaphat.

From a human perspective, I applaud Jehoshaphat for bringing an end to the civil war between Judah and Israel, which had lasted for several generations. He also continued reforms in Judah, including removing the worship of other gods and promoting the worship of Jehovah. He was a good man. The question I ask is "Was peace with Israel worth losing his son to the ways of Ahab?" In talking about what is caught versus what is taught, this story is a sober warning. Despite all the good Jehoshaphat did, when he joined Ahab in several adventures and united Jehoram to the house of Ahab through marriage, Jehoshaphat showed a tolerance of Ahab's sin that seems to have been translated to Jeroham as an approval of Ahab's lifestyle. Although the interactions with Ahab did not lead Jehoshaphat astray, it seems these interactions signaled to Jehoram that they were acceptable. We could also ask the question "Why didn't Jehoram absorb all the good things Jehoshaphat did instead of emulating Ahab?" I do not have an answer for that question, and it is a question that haunts me as a parent. I can lead a good life, but the sin I tolerate could be the stone that crushes my child. I don't write this to make us paranoid and scared to death that there might be something we are doing that is leading our child to hell, yet, I am. A warning does not mean bad things will happen, unless the warning is ignored.

I grew up being competitive in everything I did. From kickball, to math grades, or to who's the tallest, I was always striving to be better and be the best. In a balanced individual who understands the limits of that urge, this trait can be healthy. I was not that balanced person. I thought I had it under control, and it felt like an inseparable part of my personality. I even gave it credit for my successes. Then I began seeing my children displaying an intensity that mirrored how I felt inside but which I thought I had kept in check. When the three kids were arguing over a stupid, insignificant board game, with a fervor and tenacity of lion on a wildebeest, it struck me they were saying and doing things that I did, even though we had many conversations about trusting one another, the importance of sharing, realizing that value does not come from winning, and that honoring one another is more important than being the best. In short, they were manifesting my flaws, exaggerated and uglier than I thought possible. Around this time is when God showed me the story of Jehoshaphat and Jehoram, and my wife lovingly illuminated what I thought was hidden; I had the chance to repent. The way we played games started to change. I asked for their forgiveness and pointed out the behaviors we all did that were not good. We are all still very competitive, but by identifying the thing that made it poisonous, we have all been able to enjoy competitiveness without its destructive side.

On the positive side, I tried hard to get my kids to exercise with me when they were little, but something about how I did it and what I tried to teach them never stirred their interest. They wouldn't go to the pool to swim laps or do sit ups and push-ups with me, but I guess they were watching because now they are more active than I am.

In regards to what Debbie was saying about duality, I would add that, when I was younger, I thought duality was necessary to keep my world from exploding. As with the story about my epiphany in biology class, I had several things neatly separated so they would not clash with each other. I was aware that if I acknowledged this truth, then I would be ridiculed by this crowd because they believed something different. It was easier to be one way here and another way there so I did not have to deal with the possible rejection. I now recognize my fears of rejection and ridicule kept this problem alive. Allowing God to expose and treat those fears brings a singularity that involves peace and consistency, which will aid you and your children.

Do not hesitate to teach and keep talking about your passions, and displaying them, so that your children can absorb them, but, prayerfully consider the impact those passions will have on them. Allow yourself to release the version of the Lion of Judah that lives inside of you and draw your kids to join you in that place.

CHAPTER 19

SUPPORT WHAT YOU FOSTER

DEBBIE

You will find when you train your children in the truth of the gospel that they will embrace it wholeheartedly. They will not understand if they begin to see mixture in your life and may even begin to challenge you by the purity and sincerity of their faith. When my son, Joe, was in grade school, he was being bullied by another kid. This went on for a couple of years before Jerry and I found out. In fact, we only found out when we did because the bully went after a younger, smaller child and Joe stepped in between them. When he did, the bully began to punch Joe. At that point, Joe's best friend, Noah, jumped on the bully and began pounding his head. Consequently, all three fathers were called into the school office. After this all came to light, I asked Joe, "Son, why didn't you tell us you were being bullied?" His reply sent me to my knees. He said, "Mommy, Jesus says to turn the other cheek, so I've been praying for him." I was so convicted, "Oh Lord, I wanted to take the bully into the bathroom and scare the bully out of him; but Lord, my son is way more holier than I am." You see, kids just believe God. (Side note: the bully is now saved, serving God as a passionate prophet, and is one of Joe's best friends.)

When we train our children in the ways of God, we need not be surprised when they believe Him for miracles, or even if they should pray for a move of God in their generation. They may hear prophetic words that can change the path of your family. They may want to go on mission trips. Whatever God puts on their hearts, it is your job to believe God with them. Pray for them, and most important, support what you have fostered.

Now, when it comes to this chapter, the best I feel I can do is to give you some examples from our family. Your children will have different calls than my children, and therefore, God will give them different passions and dreams. The ways He will impress on your heart to support them will also come in different ways, but the important part is that you need to be there for them 100 percent.

Jerry and I both carried a dream for missions in our hearts, so it came as no surprise that all three of our children had a heart for overseas missions. In our church, we have built a strong relationship with a church family in the Philippines. As our children each reached high school age, they went on a short-term mission trip with their dad and others from our church. Each child had to work to earn the money needed to go. We hired them to do special jobs for us around the house, but also expected them to work outside of our house to earn the money. Not only did they get to experience a taste of overseas missions, but they got to experience it side-by-side with their own father.

I will tell you that over the years we have had numerous opportunities to support our children in the dreams God placed on their hearts. I will pick just one example for each child at various stages in their lives and show how it was related to the calls on their lives.

For Amy, our teacher and entrepreneur, we had the Peace Program. The Peace program was an after-school program that Amy helped a young man from our church start. They went into what was considered one of the roughest areas of Kirksville, Mo. to start an after-school program for the children of that area. For Jerry and I that meant putting our money where our mouth was. We made numerous supply run trips to help supply the program start up. We also gave to yard sales, bought T-shirts, and sponsored children involved in the program. Also, all of us in the family volunteered in one way or another. The boys were able to volunteer more than Jerry and me, but the whole family became completely involved.

Our prophetic leader with an ache in his heart to see his generation witness the presence of God, Michael, came to us in fifth grade with one of his big requests. We were at a friend's house having dinner when Mike and their two daughters came to us and said, "Mom and Dad, our church has Kingdom Kids for the younger kids and youth group for the older kids, but we feel left out. We want our own meeting where we can seek God for our age group." So Jerry and I sent them off to seek God about it and told them we would support them in whatever they heard Him leading them to do. That night Torch 360 was born. They heard God about a verse that spoke of being a torch to set fire to the surrounding area and they named the group after the verse. We began a weekly meeting in our home for fifth and sixth graders to seek God. Eventually, as these kids grew older, Torch expanded to encompass the whole high school too. In this case, supporting Michael's call meant giving our time and our home to assist the youth.

For Joseph, I've chosen a story much closer to this point in his life, even though it by no means was the first. In some ways it has been the hardest, especially for a mom. Joseph has an apostolic call on his life. Jerry and I have consequently had to support his building the church in many different fashions, but something inside of us has always known we did not have everything this boy needed. (I will go into this subject more in the next chapter.) Now, I will tell you as a preface here that out of all of my children, Joe has been the one who never wanted to leave Kirksville. He would be perfectly content to stay here the rest of his life, but God placed physical therapy in his heart as a career. However, you cannot get your doctorate in physical therapy in Kirksville, so we began the process of sending him away. Let me remind you that God never does anything for a purely monetary reason. He is all about the kingdom, always. Our group of churches has a leadership team and the main apostolic leader lives in Kansas City,

Missouri. You guessed it: Kansas City has a doctorate program for physical therapy and Joe was accepted.

You might wonder how we were able to foster this dream. Well, it started when we realized he would need to move away. First, I became a major prayer warrior over this. Next, we realized that a rule we had for Michael and Amy would not work for him. We had told all of our children we would get them through undergrad debt free, but they would have to live at home. For Joe, we realized he would need to move out his senior year in college to gain the experiences he needed to be able to move away for grad school. Once again, we opened our pocketbooks and paid for him to move out. We also helped talk him through seeking God about where to move, and finally, as we saw God draw it all together, encouraged him to seek out our friend, the apostolic leader, about where he should stay while in Kansas City. It led to Joe living with and learning from one of two men who can train him in his call in ways Jerry and I can't. In some ways, admitting you don't have everything and trusting God with your child is by far one of the hardest things to do. You see, God brought physical therapy into Joe's life, we didn't. God brought Kansas City, we didn't. God sent our friend to that city as well, we didn't. God put it on our friend's heart to take in our son, we did not. Our part was to support Joe's dreams and his ability to hear God for himself, then to let him go, no matter how difficult it was. Of course, we will continue to jump in and aid him in his transition, etc., but most importantly, we encouraged our son to go.

I hope my examples have conveyed what I was hoping to impart in this chapter. Our kids need us to not only believe God for our lives, but they need us to believe it and support them when He moves in theirs. One way my husband and I encourage each other in this is to remind ourselves that we trained our children to hear God's voice, so we need to believe and support them when they say they have.

JERRY

Debbie did a great job of describing how we were able to support our kids in the things God was bringing to them. In essence, we wanted to provide whatever we were able to provide to assist them in reaching the destinations God has for them. My goal is to describe the early and small things we did to get to the bigger things. We all realize that big things don't happen unless the little things have been done well.

A few years back, I was sitting with a friend on his couch after we had finished a nice Sunday dinner. As we were chatting about the whatever's and the what-nots, his son came running through the living room. As he dashed by his father, a cheer exploded from my friend as if his son were competing in an Olympic event. "Good job, Son! Way to go! You're flying!" I was deeply puzzled as to why he had been so enthusiastic about such an ordinary behavior. Before he caught my bewildered look, his son came back carrying an object that was necessary for whatever he and the other kids were playing. Again, my friend cheered him on: "Way to carry that toy! Good job, you almost tripped but nice recovery! Love you, Son!" My friend turned his head to make sure his son heard every word as he rocketed into the other room. When he turned back around, he was beaming with a huge smile and the satisfaction of a proud father. He stared into the distance for a while; I paused not to interrupt his moment. He finally turned back towards me with the sudden realization that he was not alone. Seeming embarrassed that he had drifted to another place, he tried to recover with the standard, "Where were we?"

My silence and bewilderment finally broke with "What was that all about?" He lifted his eyebrows, acting as if he was unaware of what I was talking about. I panned across the room with my eyes and swept my arm along his son's trajectory. "That?"

"Oh." His expression went flat then a gentle smile reorganized his face.

"Why were you making such a big deal about your son running through the room?" Although my words were flavored with sarcasm and judgment, my friend did not waver.

"Lately, I have had to correct him a lot for bad behavior and it seems like all I do is talk to him about what he is doing wrong. I know he needs that, but lately, I have been looking for any opportunity to let him know I am still his fan and that love isn't isolated to correction.

Sometimes simple things like that," sweeping his hand across the room, "are the only chances I have. I know this season of frequent correction will ease up, but I want to make sure that every day he hears encouragement for what he has done right and that he is worth more than his mistakes. It is easy to focus on the bad behaviors, to become frustrated, and to lose sight of what a blessing he is." He stopped, a huge smile covering his face, "For now, he is a good runner and a great toy carrier."

I do not remember where our conversation went from there, but that scene has played over and over in my mind a thousand times. Challenged by my friend's fervent desire for his son's success, I began to wonder how I was treating my children. Did I only talk to them when they needed correction? Did I only celebrate when they had done something outstanding? As I have pondered over this scenario, I realize it goes beyond celebration and correction; this picture touches how parents foster, or discourage, the things they are encouraging their children to pursue. If we want to develop their musical ability, we provide instruments and lessons. If reading, then we find good books for them to read. If there is an area we want to see developed in them, we invest our time and money to see it blossom. In our next book, Debbie and I talk about how we discovered these specific areas for our kids, but now I want to hone in on one that can easily slip past us.

My friend and his budding track star opened my eyes to a flaw that could have crippled my children, and I believe has injured many other children by accident. The most important thing I wanted fostered in my children was that they have a personal relationship with Jesus with an understanding and ownership of sin and salvation. I wanted them to know that Father God was approachable, that He heard every prayer, and that He always acted in ways that would be beneficial for them. The Holy Spirit, as their Comforter and Counselor, was to become a relationship that refreshed, empowered and guided them. Like most parents who want that for their kids, we took them to church and disciplined them when they sinned. Supporting what you foster in them in their relationship with God involves more than church attendance and enforcement of rules.

Proactive acknowledgment of their righteous behavior is also necessary.

Initially, I thought the path to righteousness was to avoid sin, when actually, that mindset can draw you away from Godly righteousness. When I speak of righteousness, I am referring to a spiritual condition that allows an individual to commune with God. Sin corrodes that connection, causing interaction with God to be shallow, and often adversarial. Consequently, when I tried to foster righteousness in myself, or my children, the focus was on eliminating sin. I was quick to point out every error. I sternly confronted every rebellious attitude. What was misleading is that those actions were appropriate, but since I was only trying to stomp out sin, we became frustrated because sin was never gone. It kept popping back up.

A similar mindset seems to be how fire departments started in neighborhoods across the country: Fire begins, we go put it out. After years of this approach, they realized that by the time they got to a burning building, most of the damage had been done and they were merely trying to control the fire from spreading. To improve the safety of their neighborhoods, they began to look at how fires could be prevented. Faulty electrical wiring, unsafe storage of flammable liquids, unsafe heating systems, and the easily combustible materials in couches and mattresses were regulated by local and federal agencies. They realized that preventing every fire was impossible, but with the passage of city construction codes and laws about the handling of flammable substances, their jobs began to develop from being mere hose jockeys to advocates for public safety. They began to educate the public on how to avoid starting fires and what to do to save themselves and their families in the event of a fire.

Parenting that only responds to the fire caused by sin will find that many things will be destroyed that could have been prevented. By preemptive examination of how our children are wired, how they handle combustible situations, and teaching them how to respond to fire, we are training them to shift away from fire control (avoidance of sin) and to move towards fire prevention (a healthy relationship with God).

The goal of being sinless is admirable but naive, and it is not the path to building a good connection with God. Let's review a few verses.

Colossians 2:20-23. (NIV)

> Since you died with Christ to the elemental spiritual
> forces of this world, why, as though you still belonged
> to the world, do you submit to its rules: "Do not
> handle! Do not taste! Do not touch!"? These rules,
> which have to do with things that are all destined to
> perish with use, are based on merely human
> commands and teachings. Such regulations indeed
> have an appearance of wisdom, with their self-
> imposed worship, their false humility and their harsh
> treatment of the body, but they lack any value in
> restraining sensual indulgence.

Paul is challenging the Colossians concerning how they are pursuing their new life in God. If they have been redeemed, now living in the power of God, why are they trying to develop human systems to improve their righteousness? These things may appear wise, but they are harsh to the body and have no value in controlling sinful pursuits.

Paul elaborates for the Ephesians that working to gain salvation is worthless; it is a gift given, not a reward earned.

Ephesians 2:8-9. (ESV)

> For by grace you have been saved through faith. And this
> is not your own doing; it is the gift of God, not a
> result of works, so that no one may boast.

The work of avoiding sin, trying to earn righteousness, seeking to reside in the grace that saves is not something we accomplish; it is something we receive.

Jesus also confronted this mindset in John chapter six. He has admonished the crowds following him to not work for free food but to seek eternal life. They asked, "What must we do to do the works God requires?" (John 6:28. NIV). How shall we direct our efforts so that we can have this positive relationship with God? How do we gain God's approval and enter into eternal life?

John 6:29. (NIV)

> Jesus answered, "The work of God is this: to believe in
> the one he has sent."

Like Paul's words to the Colossians, there is no mention of the rules. Jesus gives the starting point that Paul elaborates in the Ephesian's letter: Salvation, the removal of the sin that kept us from God, is a gift to those who want a relationship with Him.

Returning to our children, if we short-sightedly focus on their sin, we are only teaching them how to put out fires. Fire prevention comes from fostering their ability to believe in the One who was sent. As a relationship is built with Jesus, the desire to sin diminishes significantly. The deeper we are engulfed in His love and grace, the less attractive are the things that would separate us from Him. This mindset is what we want to foster in our children and support it with our words and actions. To foster this relationship with Jesus in our children, we need to model my friend: Watch for opportunities to cheer for them as they step into their own relationship with Jesus.

In our house it looked something like this: The three of them were playing a game, not so quietly, in a corner of the living room. As the volume increased, I began to pay attention more closely to their conversation.

"Amy, you can't do that? It was my turn and you skipped me!"

"It says here in the rules that I can." Being the only one of the three that had the reading ability to comprehend the rules, her declaration was beyond dispute. "Joe, stop taking my money!"

"It was my money. It fell into your pile when Michael bumped the board."

With her right hand, Amy swung the rule book at Michael like a sword, while her left hand was trying to reclaim from Joe the disputed money. Michael defiantly rolled the dice to take his turn. Through gritted teeth and the glare of an angry Rottweiler, Michael growled, "Amy, stop hitting me." Meanwhile, in the confusion, it appeared Joe was using the distraction to his advantage until he reached across the board to grab something that Michael thought belonged to him. "Joe, stop!"

I am not sure if it was Joe leaning across the board, or Michael swatting at Joe's hand, or if one of Amy's swings of the rule book did it, but the game board flipped in the air and pieces went flying everywhere. Pandemonium broke out, full of accusations and yelling. At this point, I stepped in with the normal dad inquisition, "What's going on?" while giving the glare that works like Wonder Woman's lasso of truth. My presence brought a moment of silence, which passed like the calm before the storm, allowing them to catch their breath to release the tornado of indictments of cheating, felonious assault, money laundering, and theft. Not having the wisdom of Solomon to discern the offenders and the offended, I did the next best thing, time out. "Michael, the dining room. Amy, the guest bedroom. Joe, the stairs. No talking. No playing. I want you to think about what happened here and in a few minutes you will come back, pick up the pieces, and start the game over. You will not argue and you will consider your siblings more important than winning. You will come back when everybody has changed their face." ("Change your face" is a Burbee-ism we developed when they were toddlers, when they had no idea what it meant to "Change your attitude." Most toddlers have not developed the ability to hide their emotions and what they are feeling is written plainly on their face. When they changed their face, we knew they had changed their attitude. Debbie and I continue to use it to this day.)

After a few minutes I made my rounds through the guest bedroom, the stairs, and the dining room to check faces. I asked them what they were going to do differently this time, how they wanted to be treated, and how did Jesus want them to play together. When the storm had passed, I called them back into the living room. "Pick it up and start over." I lingered as they put it back together and watched the first couple of rounds, then exited stage right, still listening from a distance. Occasionally, I would have to bark, "Hey! What's going on?" when the volume would rise. Eventually, the game moved along smoothly.

That was the correction portion of fostering them to live as Jesus lives, loving each other and thinking more highly of the other than of themselves. The supporting part came when I walked by a few minutes later and said, "How's it going?" Usually with gleeful faces they would recount who was winning and all the good moves. To support what I was fostering I would praise them for changing their faces and playing well together. "Good job, guys."

As time would pass, and similar storms would arise, we would have correction and praise, but always seeking to balance them in a manner that supported what we were fostering in them. More importantly, I would look for chances to promote actions that reflected a deepening of their relationship with God. These ranged from talking about Bible reading, sermons, and thought-provokers I would throw at them, but the ones that were a bit more difficult to see were the changes in their behavior, like the ones that were made during the game. "Michael, thanks for helping to carry Amy's stuff to the car." "Joe, that was kind of you to trade your lunch snack with Amy because she didn't like the one she had. I know you would have rather kept it for yourself. That's being like Jesus, good job." "Amy, thanks for helping Joe find a clean shirt this morning. I could hear how frustrated he was getting and you did a great job helping to calm things down. Thank you."

Everyday I wanted to encourage the behaviors that reflected what Debbie and I had wanted to see developed in them. I was initially afraid that if I praised them in the midst of a correction that they would think I was approving of their poor attitudes or reckless behaviors. I found that if I clearly identified what I was praising and what I was correcting, the balance remained intact. There was plenty of correction, which is love, but praising them built a deeper relationship in that love. We wanted them to build that type of relationship with Jesus, and by modeling how He corrected and praised us, we felt we were opening the door that would lead them there. I found that if I wanted to foster righteousness in my children, focusing on how wonderful their relationship with Jesus could be was equally supportive as disciplining their sin. Support their active pursuit of Jesus, which is fostered out of our love for God and our love for them.

CHAPTER 20
MOVING ON TO THE NEXT BOOK

DEBBIE

As we reach the last chapter in this book, I truly hope you have learned a lot from our life experiences and the stories we have felt led to share with you. I also hope you liked this book enough to at least have a curiosity about the next two books and want to keep traveling on this journey with us. When we set out to write a book on parenting, it was just that, one book on parenting. It wasn't until we were almost finished with that book and began to get feedback from some trusted friends, advisors, and our children that we realized maybe one book was not sufficient to cover all we needed to share. My son-in-love put it this way: it feels like you're trying to stuff everything you can at us in one attempt (my paraphrase due to poor memory of his exact phrasing). I guess he really wasn't that far off either, because the more I talked with young parents and heard their fears and needs when it came to parenting, the more I was determined to give them everything I could to help in any way possible.

Parenting is not as easy as they sometimes make it sound. These precious little bundles of joy do not come with a set of instructions. The fan for your bedroom probably came with at least ten pages of instructions, and some of them were probably in multiple languages. But little humans are not sent home from the hospital with any manuals, and some of you did not have the best role models to learn from. So yes, I thought if I only had one shot at this, then I better give you the whole load. Raising our children in the kingdom of God is extremely important. Their lives depend on us doing the best we can for them.

The original book was broken up into three sections which we condensed into the first book minus a lot of extra explanation for the process. So books 2 and 3 are the rest of the explanation. Book 2, which is titled "What I Have I Give To You", is the really important one in my opinion. In book 2, we want to tell you how we went about determining which things we felt were the important things we needed to train our children in and why. We know when we say that you are tasked with training your children in the ways of God that all of you probably thought of the obvious topics, like prayer and the Bible. But training a child in the way they need to go in this life is so much more than just that. Those things are vital to our Christian walk, but they are barely scratching the surface of the vast topics so important to your child's success.

In book 2, Jerry and I tell you how we decided on the topics that were important for us to train our children in and why we felt each was vital, especially in this culture and time period we live in. You, of course, will have to be in unity with your spouse about the topics you feel are important for your family, but I am sure that this next book will cause you to broaden your scope and see the immensity of all a parent is tasked with. We try hard to explain our reasoning, and we realize some of the things that are important to us you may have not thought about in the way we explain them.

Jerry has a saying that basically says the things that come easy to you may not come easy to someone else, and if it is easy for you, you often do not even know that someone else may not understand it like you do. Stated more simply, because you understand something doesn't mean everyone else does too. As a nurse, it was always a little amusing to me to watch a doctor work really hard in medical terms to describe to a patient what was going on in their care. Then after the doctor left the room to have the patient look at me and say, "What did he say?" It became so common that I wouldn't leave the room with the doctor there alone because I knew the patient did not understand a word he said. I became very good at speaking to people about their bodies in a language I knew they already understood or by explaining in very basic terms. The doctors were not trying to talk over a patients head, but the language of medicine they used in every part of their lives had become so clear to them that they did not realize that it was like a foreign language to their patients.

I tell you all of that because we do not want to assume any of the insights that God gave us will be as clear to you as it might have been to us. So we even in some chapters explain what we mean by the concepts we felt were vital for our children to understand. Training up your child in the way he should go so that when he gets older he will not depart from it is such an important promise for us in God's Word. We didn't want to miss out on even one part of that promise for our children, and we are sure you don't either.

Book 3, titled " Train up A Child In The Way He Shoulld Go" is a more practical guide on how we trained our children in each of the topics we chose. It is a book filled with more practical applications on the topics and some great stories about the fun we had training our children. The stage of life Jerry and I are in right now is exciting because every season with God is amazing, but I would be lying if I didn't say that raising children God's way was such an amazing experience and so fun that I sometimes miss those days with every fiber of my being. My desire for you is that you, like me, will be able to say that your house is a house of blessing because of the children who grew up in it and the amazing adults they have become.

JERRY

The next book is titled *What I Have I Give You* in which we discuss things we felt were important for our kids to gain from us and what we want to give you. We mostly discuss topics of character that we felt were necessary for our kids to see demonstrated in us and that we needed to train them to incorporate into their lifestyles. As a young parent, I did not realize I was the major force that established foundational elements, like identity and value, in my children, which in turn influenced how my children defined themselves and their feelings of worth. As I interact with people, I have been astounded by the deficiencies in these two elements and the devastation it brings to their lives. Somehow, mom and dad did not communicate to this person how unique and important they are. We cannot let our children leave home in that condition.

Two other important chapters discuss taking responsibility for your actions and not being defined by your sin, both being areas that shipwreck many people. "It's not my fault" or "I can never change" are two phrases that have no place in the Christian vocabulary, yet understanding the intricacies of these lies is easily missed.

As Debbie mentioned, the topics in the next book are ones that were important to us and we present them to you to stir ideas, not to declare we found the perfect template for forming a child. Still, we challenge you to consider them. The concepts from this first book lay a foundation on how to seek God for the pattern for your children, and the next book is the result of our intercessions and how we perceived them.

Hopefully, we have answered the question *What Do We Do With God's Best Gift?*, and you have found the footing to stand firm in faith-established confidence that you have what it takes to parent your child. God has your back, and He is more than eager to help. Let's move forward in this same confidence, continue to grow in God, and boldly proclaim to your children, *What I Have I Give You.*

NOTE FROM THE AUTHORS

We hope you enjoyed this book.

Please send us any thoughts or questions you may have. We would like to hear what God has stirred in your heart and the ideas and insights you have received from Him for your children.

If you reply, we will be adding you to our email list to let you know of any future books we write, merchandise offers, more suggestions, and some of the responses we have received (anonymous and identity concealed).

If you would like to comment, but do not want to be on the email list, please mention that in your reply.

Or, if you would prefer not to have your comments published, please let us know that as well.

May God continue to bless you and your children.

Debbie and Jerry
DebbieJerry88@gmail.com

ACKNOWLEDGMENTS

We thank God, because without His constant guidance, we know we could not have accomplished raising children that love Him, nor been able to write a book about it.

We also want to thank all the faithful men and women of God from our local church who loved and poured into our children throughout their childhood. Thank you for loving them with us.

ABOUT THE AUTHORS

Shortly after getting married, Debbie and Jerry moved to Kirksville, Missouri, so Jerry could attend medical school, but soon discovered that God also had brought them to a loving church family. For over thirty years they have served God in various capacities within the church having led small group meetings, served the youth in all age groups, and passionately shared their pastoral hearts to help build God's Kingdom in a way that brings glory to His name. Debbie has worked as a nurse, teacher, and business owner, while Jerry has worked in the emergency department of the local hospital. Debbie's gift for hospitality has allowed them to have people from all over the world spend time in their home. Both have a heart for the church world wide and Jerry has been able to take each of the children to the Philippines to experience the Lord's church in a different culture.

Debbie enjoys all types of crafting, including cross stitch and jewelry making. Both have developed a love for leather work, especially making various types of bags and purses. Jerry enjoys music, playing several instruments and having written several songs, including the songs for a bluegrass band he and his daughter played in several years ago. While the children were young, most of their time was spent at every game, practice, or performance cheering for their kids. All three children graduated from the local university, and two have completed doctoral programs. Two marriages and two grandchildren have increased the size of their family, as well as adding more love and fun.

When they became empty nesters, they asked God not to retire them, but to keep them working full-time in His Kingdom. He answered by continuing them in the discipling of others, opening the doors to writing, and bringing more people into their home. Their joy for travel has allowed Debbie to see the amazing Sistine Chapel and Jerry to salmon fish in Alaska. They both believe that if they don't put limits on God, there is no end to the adventures and experiences He will bring to them. They look forward to what He brings in the future.

COMING SOON FROM JERRY AND DEBBIE BURBEE

BOOK TWO: WHAT I HAVE, I GIVE TO YOU

Acts 3:6 (NIV)

"...what I do have I give you, In the name of Jesus Christ..."

BOOK THREE: TRAIN UP A CHILD IN THE WAY TO GO

Humorous adventures of training a child

Made in the USA
Monee, IL
23 August 2023